FITNESS
WALKING

Jeff Bolles

University of North Carolina, Pembroke

Kendall Hunt
publishing company

Kendall Hunt
publishing company

www.kendallhunt.com
Send all inquiries to:
4050 Westmark Drive
Dubuque, IA 52004-1840

ISBN 978-1-4652-9642-9

Printed in the United States of America

CONTENTS

INTRODUCTION

Why Walk?

Walking is a human being's first experience in evolved locomotion. When taking his first steps, a toddler gains a sense of independence and the key to unlocking adventures never before imagined. Walking is almost as essential as breathing, yet it often does not receive any consideration, especially with respect to walking with the purpose of improving one's physical health. This book is dedicated to exploring how walking for fitness can be the foundation of an active and healthy lifestyle.

Fitness walking is one of the most enjoyable and inexpensive forms of exercise available. Walking is limitless, as a person can walk just about anywhere at just about any time of day. There is no need for special equipment; one does not need any type of membership, and a person does not have to sweat a lot to get some benefits from walking. Working full-time? Use two fifteen-minute breaks to total a half hour of heart-healthy exercise. Turn a lunch hour into a power hour spending the time not used for eating to walk. Alternatively, if one wants to wind down from a long day at the office, parking the vehicle in the garage and heading for the streets before even walking through the door can be very restorative. In short, fitness walking is convenient and effective and offers tremendous opportunities for improving one's cardiovascular fitness while providing an outlet for relieving stress.

More than being a terrific way to exercise, walking can increase a person's social network. Walking groups can be found just about anywhere, and if there is not one close by, it is very easy to get one started. Calling a coworker and asking him or her to go for a walk to catch up is both physically and socially healthy. Making the next meeting of a committee or workgroup into a walking meeting is a terrific change of pace that may lead to creative and innovative approaches never before considered. Try navigating the work or college campus by walking, rather than driving. A regular fitness walking routine will very likely lead to new observations and opportunities simply out of the experiences and environments that are presented.

New to a neighborhood? Start walking. Not only will a person quickly learn more about the surrounding environment, but it is a great way to quickly establish relationships with the neighbors. Especially for those who have relocated to a new area, taking walks around the neighborhood provides limitless opportunities to meet and interact with others in the community. One may even meet a neighbor or two who want to start joining in the walk, which will support one's regular walking and can lead to increased efficacy and progressive goal setting (see Chapter Nine).

How to Use This Book

While walking is a basic and inherent skill, the art of walking for fitness requires some additional knowledge. This book covers important topics including proper warm-up and cool-down measures, improving cardiovascular health with advanced walking routines, increasing strength and stamina through resistance training, and meeting body composition goals through appropriate dietary consumption.

In addition to providing content on the topics expressed above, this book provides case study examples. The case studies should make even greater sense of the concepts expressed in the general text. Further, timely tips can help reinforce a concept expressed in the reading, or a tip might present a novel idea that is not expressed in the general text.

Further application of the book's content is available by completing the "In Practice" exercises. Those exercises ask the reader to employ the concepts and actions that are defined in the text, providing the opportunity to gain a greater perspective of one's current practices, limitations, and expectations.

This text should be a dynamic guide to developing a healthy lifestyle that revolves around fitness walking, a lifestyle that is solely limited by one's aspirations and expectations.

© Shutterstock/Blazej Lyjak

Figure 1.1 The benefits and opportunities made available through a fitness walking lifestyle are limitless.

TECHNOLOGY AND EQUIPMENT FOR WALKING

Introduction

When it comes to any exercise, an exerciser needs to be comfortable, safe, and well equipped. Respective to walking, it is critical that clothing and shoes are chosen to prevent blisters, chaffing, and pressure points. Clothing needs to allow for efficient thermoregulation (balancing hot and cold), while shoes need to allow for or facilitate normal gait, be flexible, supportive, and well cushioned. One should also use equipment that promotes safety while exercising, and using a tracking tool can help to chart progress, improve goal setting, and discover the source of joint injury or discomfort.

This chapter will inform the readers of the advances in clothing technology and how they help control heat loss and gain. Further, the chapter will discuss which shoes are most appropriate for walkers of all different body proportions and mechanics. Finally, this chapter will discuss tools that promote safety and allow for tracking progress.

Clothing

Regardless of the workout, a person needs to be comfortable when exercising. Therefore, it is important to wear clothing that not only fits well but also aids in performance. Modern workout gear is designed to move sweat off the body and increase ventilation in order to improve thermoregulation. Additionally, today's workout clothing is designed to reduce friction, lessening the wearer's likelihood of becoming chaffed.

Thermoregulation is critical to exercise performance, in both hot ($\geq 80°F$) and cold ($\leq 40°F$) environments. As stated earlier, thermoregulation is the balance of hot and cold, meaning that the body is maintaining a thermo-neutral temperature (relatively close to 98.6°F). Thermo-neutrality is maintained by releasing body heat in hot environments and retaining body heat in cold environments, and much of that is accomplished through the circulation of blood from the body's core to the surface of the skin and back again.

In the heat, proper thermoregulation requires the transfer of heat into the environment (the air surrounding the body). When internal body temperatures increase, the hypothalamus directs the heat regulatory glands of the body (mainly the pituitary and thyroid glands) to stimulate sweating. By sweating, the body is exposing moisture to the outside environment. That water then evaporates, giving off heat energy and cooling the skin. As blood passes under the cooled skin, it also cools. The cooler blood then returns to the core of the body, where it cools the organs while picking up more heat itself. As long as there is sufficient water to produce sweat, this process continues to cool the body and allows for continuation of the athletic endeavor.

© Shutterstock/mimagephotography

Figure 2.1 Exercising without a shirt is less effective than using moisture-wicking clothing that facilitates evaporation.

There are challenges to the body's ability to dissipate heat. When exercising in a humid environment, the air is already heavily saturated with moisture, decreasing the evaporation of sweat. If sweat does not evaporate (it just rolls off the skin), there is no heat exchange, and the body does not cool as described above. With the body not cooling as it needs to, the hypothalamus increases sweat production in an effort to increase heat loss. However, with the air still saturated, there is little change in evaporation. The increased sweating decreases blood volume, which negatively affects cardiovascular performance. The decreased performance leads to the exerciser working harder to maintain the same intensity, leading to increased body temperatures and a deadly spiral of increased heat production and decreased fluid levels. The prudent exerciser will stop exercising, thereby decreasing metabolic heat production and allowing the body to cool. The more obstinate exerciser will push on, eventually collapsing due to heat exhaustion and putting himself or herself at risk of heat stroke or death.

One of the more common practices of those exercising in the heat is to exercise without a shirt (more common in runners than walkers). The belief is that increasing the amount of skin exposed to the air will increase evaporation and body cooling, and it works while the sweat rate is fairly light. However, by exposing more skin to the environment, the exerciser is also allowing more skin to directly absorb the heat energy from the Sun's radiation, decreasing the overall cooling of the skin. As body temperatures increase, sweat rate increases, and the higher rate of sweat exceeds the rate of evaporation. This leads to the sweat simply rolling off the skin, and there is little cooling. Thus, by not wearing a shirt, the exerciser is contributing to increased body temperature.

Most athletic clothing is now made of synthetic fibers that pull moisture off the skin, taking the heat energy with it. The sweat-soaked clothing then exposes the moisture to the environment, where it can evaporate into the atmosphere, cooling the fabric. The fabric will be further cooled by the convective cooling coming from the flow of the cooler air as generated by the exerciser's movement. The cooled fabric then cools the skin and blood. In addition to the conductive effect of the cooled fabric touching the skin, the air between the body and the fabric is also cooled, providing a convective layer of cooler air that also aids in decreasing body temperature.

Tip 2.1

In normal environments, human beings lose the majority of their body heat through evaporation. In order to maintain fluid balance, exercisers need to drink 6–8 ounces of water for every 15 minutes of exercise.

The convection effect is increased when one uses moisture-wicking compression apparel that molds tightly to the body. The compression layer transfers the sweat directly to an outer layer, thereby creating a moist outer layer. With both evaporation and convection acting on the fabric, the fabric is considerably cooler than the skin. The compression layer resists clinging to the outer layer, more so than the skin does, creating a more pronounced layer of cooler air between the skin and the outer garment, offering the greater convective cooling as suggested above.

In addition to the thermoregulation offered by today's workout wear, the new materials are more comfortable than traditional cotton fabrics. Compared to cotton clothing, moisture-wicking material stays drier and clings to the skin less, making it less likely to cause friction. Decreased friction between the clothing and the skin reduces chaffing and general discomfort. When combining the thermoregulation and comfort benefits that come from wearing moisture-wicking clothing, it is quite apparent that moisture-wicking clothing is optimal for exercise in the heat.

Today's technologically superior workout clothing also helps to regulate body temperatures in colder weather. One of the challenges of dressing for cold weather activity is to ensure that one stays warm while not overheating. The thinner, lighter moisture-wicking clothes that aid in warm weather thermoregulation are invaluable in cold weather thermoregulation as well.

It's well advertised that it is best to dress in layers for colder weather. Dressing in layers provides two distinct benefits to the cold weather exerciser. First, by dressing in layers, multiple pockets of air are formed between the clothes. Because those pockets of air are protected from the outside air, they get progressively warmer as they near the body, thereby helping to conserve body heat. Second, if the exerciser begins to get too warm, shedding a layer of clothing will allow for greater evaporation, providing a bit more cooling. Additionally, removing a layer leads to one less air pocket being formed and slightly less warmth being held in by the inner air pockets.

There is a science to layering clothes for cold weather. The layer closest to the skin should be a moisture-wicking, tight-fitting material that will pull sweat away from the body and move it to an outer layer where it can evaporate. The second layer should be a looser moisture-wicking layer that will allow for evaporation. If it is extremely cold, a third layer, one that provides some insulation, should be added. Finally, the outer layer should protect against wind while still providing breathability (e.g. a vented jacket shell).

Shoes

Probably of greatest importance in any walker's wardrobe are the shoes that she puts on her feet. Walking shoes should be supportive yet flexible, well cushioned yet stable, and light weight yet well built. Some shoe manufacturers still make shoes specifically designed for walking. However, the best shoes for fitness walking are running shoes. Because running shoes feature great cushioning, good flexibility, and substantial support, a walker should be able to perform proficiently and comfortably in walks of any distance or speed. As well, running shoes come in a variety of styles and features, which are critical to getting the right shoe for one's foot.

Figure 2.2 The semi-curved last is the most common in running shoes.

Of critical importance, once must understand the structure of a running shoe. Knowing how a running shoe is designed will allow a walker make the right decision on the right shoe for his or her biomechanical and cushioning needs. The first consideration should be the last of the shoe. The last is the shoe's foundation. A shoe's last should be considered from two different respects, the shape and the construction.

A shoe's last is typically shaped in one of three ways. The most popular is the semi-curved last, which features a slight curve toward the inside (big toe) part of the foot. The most stable last is the straight last, which has virtually no curve, as the name implies. Finally, the least popular shape for a last is the curved shape. A curved last has a fairly exaggerated curve toward the inside of the foot.

In order to determine the shape of a shoe's last, look at the bottom of the shoe, drawing an imaginary line up the middle of the shoe, from the heel to the toe. If the shoe is equidistant on either side of the midline and the middle of the shoe's toe is in line with the midline, the shoe is straight lasted. If the shoe curves more to the inside of the shoe, the last is semi-curved. If most of the toe of the shoe is to the inside part of the shoe, meaning that the fourth and fifth toe areas of the toe box are in the midline part of the shoe, the shoe is built on a curved last. The different shaped lasts are designed to meet the needs of people with different shaped feet.

The semi-curved last is the most popular shape for running and walking shoes, as it is the appropriate last for people who have low to moderately high arches, the most common arch types. The semi-curved last promotes a neutral foot strike, which allows the foot to roll from heel to toe as the mechanics of walking require (see Chapter Five). Often, devices are built into the midsole of the shoe, in order to provide additional support where an exerciser might need it (see below).

Typically, unless a person over-pronates (the foot rolls toward the inside of the foot) or over-supinates (the foot rolls toward the outside of the foot; also called under-pronation), the semi-curved last provides the best fit. For those who over-pronate, which typically coincides with somebody having flat feet, the straight last is best. A straight-lasted shoe has a flat, wide base that resists an inward roll of the shoe and resists over-pronation. Straight-lasted shoes offer the most motion control, and they should be considered essential for those who pronate heavily. Conversely, the curved last works best for those people with high arches, as they tend to over-supinate. The curved last promotes an inward roll of the foot, promoting a push off the big toe as is required for a normal gait. Curved lasts are most common in high-performance running shoes used for racing. They offer the least stability and motion control and promote the rapid toe-off associated with high-performance locomotion.

The construction of the last is also of critical importance. Generally, there are three ways a last is constructed, which are board-lasted, slip-lasted, and combination-lasted. The board last is exactly as the name implies. The manufacturer uses a stiff piece of cardboard to join the insole to the midsole. The cardboard provides support to the foot and increases the stability (resistance to rolling) and stiffness (less forefoot flexibility) of the shoe. The board last is easily recognized by pulling out the insole and observing the hard board running from toe to heel. A slip last is provided by the manufacturer simply sewing the two pieces of the shoe's upper together and attaching the upper to the midsole. Slip lasts allow for the greatest forefoot flexibility in a shoe, and the absence of the additional board material makes the shoe much lighter. A slip last will appear as stitched fabric running from the toe to the heel. A combination last provides a board last in the heel of the shoe and slip lasting from the midfoot of the shoe forward. Combination-lasted shoes provide stability at the point of impact (if impact is made at the heel [see Chapter Five]) and the flexibility of a slip last at the forefoot. Due to the combination of support and responsiveness that they provide, combination lasts are the most popular type of last construction.

The midsole is just as important as the last of the shoe. The midsole is the part of the shoe in which the manufacturer supplies the cushioning, additional motion control mechanisms, and the foam that supports the shoe. Shoe manufacturers will use different varieties and densities of foams when constructing their shoes. EVA foam is very popular, as it is light weight and yet very tough. Many companies often employ duo-density foam construction in their midsoles, using a denser foam on the outside of the midsole (for stability) and a less dense foam on the inside, which can provide a bit more dissipation of the shock created at impact, as well as lessening the weight of the midsole.

━━━ Tip 2.2 ━━━

To get a better understanding of your typical gait pattern, take a good look at your shoes. Take a well-worn pair of shoes and place them on a table (make sure the laces are tucked into the shoes). Get eye-level to the back of the shoes and look at the heel counter. If the heel counter is straight up and down (including the top fabric), that shoe was a good one for you. If the heel counter is falling to the inside of the shoe, you are pronating, and you should consider a shoe to correct pronation. If your heel counter is falling to the outside of the shoe, you are supinating, and you should consider a shoe that controls for supination a bit more.

In addition to the foams companies use in their midsoles, they also provide pieces that correct mechanical errors in one's foot strike. Although the devices and methods employed by the companies vary, the most popular corrective insert is a medial post. Some companies will make medial posts out of a very dense foam, while many use lightweight, rigid, plastics. Some companies place the medial posts only at the heel, while others will have posts that run from the heel to the arch or even the base of the metatarsals. Heel-based posts do little to control biomechanical deficiencies in runners who strike at the midfoot forward, while medial posting that runs all the way from heel to the metatarsal arch is more restrictive. Because of the variations in design and control, it is best to seek expert fitting experts when trying to find a shoe that corrects for biomechanical needs. Try to solicit the help of a shoe fitting expert at a specialty running shoe store, and once you find the right shoe, it is best not to change it until the manufacturer does something to force your hand.

Another aspect of the midsole is the cushioning agent that is used. Some companies simply rely on the foam to provide the cushioning, while most use some sort of material to absorb impact and provide cushioning. Popular cushioning agents are encapsulated air or water, gel-infused pads, plastic pieces that collapse and reform on impact and release, and plastic devices that spread the impact throughout the midsole.

The final piece of a shoe's foundation is the outsole or as it is more commonly called, the sole. Typically, soles are made up of tire-grade rubber and can stand up to more than 600 miles of walking or running. Manufacturers are getting more creative with outsoles now, and instead of using full rubber pieces that cover the entire bottom of the shoe, some companies are using pieces of rubber in the high contact parts of the sole while cutting away the midsole in the uncovered parts. This practice decreases the weight of the shoe while also increasing the flexibility of the forefoot.

Some shoes, those that are made for running on trails, will feature thicker and chunkier rubber soles. These soles are designed to withstand piercing from rocks that might be encountered on the trails, while also providing the traction necessary to gain a foothold in the soft dirt often encountered while on trail runs. Because of the friction they can generate, trail shoes should not be used on roads. The increased friction can lead to musculoskeletal injuries.

Safety

Walking on the roads can be somewhat risky, as one must share the road with vehicles. Drivers can often become distracted, taking their focus off objects in their car's paths. As well, walker can sometimes blend in with other things on the road, making them fairly inconspicuous to approaching drivers. As well, different environmental features, including lighting, weather factors, and blind spots, can put a walker at risk for not being seen. A walker should take advantage of every opportunity to make himself or herself as visible to oncoming traffic as possible.

Reflective materials are often built into exercise apparel, especially in shoes and outerwear. However, that little bit of reflective material is often not enough to attract the attention of oncoming drivers. Reflective vests provide a lot of reflective surface area and are at a height that will be in the direct line of sight of most drivers. Arm and leg bands are also good options, as they attach to moving limbs, and that movement will make them more conspicuous. Running and walking hats also come with reflective material added. Finally, for exercise during cooler seasons, many companies are now producing hats and gloves that have reflective material built into them.

Reflective pieces are not the only options for promoting safety. Several versions of clip-on lights are being produced for exercisers. Some lights are made to clip on clothing and offer various flashing patterns that can be used to catch the attention of oncoming drivers. Other devices are designed be used as headlights that can be mounted on hats or strapped around the head with a headband. There are also smaller lights that are designed to be clipped on shoelaces.

Safety is not just about being seen on the road. Many walkers choose to walk alone. Carrying devices designed to deter attackers might also be appropriate. For those who walk alone, especially females, carrying a container of mace or pepper spray, or even an electric shock device, should be a strong consideration.

© Shutterstock/Stefan Holm

Figure 2.3 Reflective vests can save a life! Wearing reflective material will substantially increase one's visibility while exercising at night.

Walking alone also leaves one without help should a tragedy occur. An accident or illness can leave a person incapacitated while on the roadside. Especially for those who might have a medical condition, it is highly recommended that an ID bracelet that contains an emergency contact and any allergies be worn with every walk. There are many companies that can provide such bracelets, and a simple Internet search for running ID bracelets should generate multiple options.

Tracking

Fitness tracking is a multi-billion-dollar industry that is gaining momentum. Activity trackers are becoming increasingly popular, with many sporting designs that make them indistinguishable as anything but jewelry. As well, activity trackers are providing the user with more and more useful feedback, including activity levels, calories burned, steps climbed, minutes of activity, and hours and quality of sleep. Many trackers also provide the opportunity to interact and compete with other people who use the same device.

The price tag on some fitness trackers can be somewhat prohibitive. Additionally, some trackers are not water resistant, limiting their usefulness in water environments. Fitness-tracking devices can range from just over ten dollars to hundreds of dollars, and many of the high-priced devices provide functionality that rivals smart watches. However, there are also smart watches that are much less expensive than the high-priced fitness trackers, so one must do his or her due diligence in considering all pros and cons of the tracker against the price. Another consideration that must be made is that there is substantial lack of resilience with regard to using activity trackers. An astounding number of users (often reported at over 50%) stop using fitness trackers within three months of beginning their use.

Because smart watches offer similar features to activity trackers, plus many additional features, they may be better options than a simple fitness tracker. Smart phones also provide options for tracking fitness. There are many great smart phone apps that use GPS satellites to accurately record distances traveled and the time spent exercising.

Regardless of the way in which a walker tracks his or her activity, using a form of tracking can provide valuable feedback that can be used to adjust training (see Chapters Six and Seven); establish neutral, negative, or positive caloric balances (see Chapter Eight); and set goals to help maintain a healthy lifestyle practice (see Chapter Nine).

© Shutterstock/Syda Productions

Figure 2.4 Fitness trackers can provide motivation and important feedback for workouts. However, it is important to research all options to determine which device is most appropriate for you.

Conclusion

There are many different advances that allow a walker to exercise safely, effectively, and comfortably. Much of what was presented in this chapter is open to subjectivity, meaning that the exerciser should have plenty to consider in making his or her choices. It is, however, recommended that the exerciser take advantage of expert advice in making such decisions.

In Practice

It is important to know what you are wearing. Use an online shoe store (roadrunnersports.com is a good one) to research the shoes that you are walking in, completing the following table.

Name of Shoe	
Last Shape	
Last Construction	
Midsole Foam	
Midsole Cushioning	
Midsole Gait Adjustment Piece	
Weight of Shoe	
Classification of Shoe (Stability, Performance, Neutral, etc.)	
Your Evaluation of Your Shoe (Is it the right shoe for you? Why or why not?)	

TESTING YOUR FITNESS

Introduction

Fitness walking is generally performed in order to bring about improved cardiovascular fitness. However, to get the most out of fitness walking, one must embrace all of the variables that make up physical fitness. It is critical to have baseline measures of fitness, so as to fully appreciate where one's fitness is at. As well, regular repetition of those same measures provides feedback on progress and the realization of established goals.

There are six components to physical fitness: body composition, flexibility, muscular strength, muscular power, muscular endurance, and aerobic power (cardiovascular capacity). Testing for each of those components offers the exerciser a complete analysis of his or her current fitness status. There are many tests one can perform to test each of the six components of fitness, some of which require extravagant equipment and others require very little to no equipment at all. Some tests are more accurate than others, as well.

While there are many ways to test for each fitness component, each with its strengths and weaknesses, the most important aspect of monitoring one's progress is to use the same test each and every time. This chapter focuses on one simple test for each of the six components as listed, with the exception of muscular endurance, for which there are two tests presented.

Body Composition

There are many ways in which body composition can be tested. However, most of those methods cannot be measured by oneself. Certainly a person cannot test his or her body composition using the gold standard methods of hydrostatic weighing or the Bod Pod. As well, one is not able to pinch himself or herself as required to perform a body fat analysis with skinfold testing. That leaves only one realistic, viable option. That option is bioelectrical impedance (BIA).

BIA works by way of the machine sending a very low-strength electric impulse through the body. The impulse is not strong enough to be felt, and it presents no harm to the body. However, the impulse can be heavily influenced by the composition of the blood. Therefore, it is critical that a person is normally hydrated, has not eaten in at least two hours, and has not exercised in two hours.

There are many different types of BIA testing units available, all with varying degrees of accuracy. Lab-oriented models are too expensive and require the subject to lie still, so they are not appropriate for independent monitoring of body fat. However, there are a number of excellent BIA bathroom scales on the market, with price usually being indicative of accuracy and quality. Those who are serious about being healthy should not settle for a BIA scale that regularly costs less than $100. Because each scale will have different procedures, a person using a BIA scale should follow the directions that

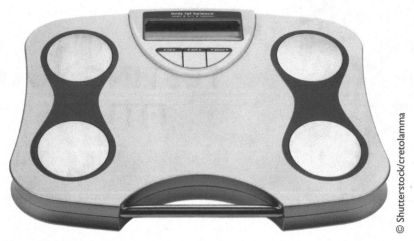

© Shutterstock/cretolamma

Figure 3.1 Body composition scales are readily identifiable by the electrode plates upon which one places the feet. For best results, be sure to clean the feet and the scale with rubbing alcohol, prior to testing.

came with the unit. However, abstaining from food and exercise for two hours prior to the test is a standard protocol that should be followed. As well, ensuring one is normally hydrated is critical to receiving valid feedback.

Appropriate body composition levels vary by sex, with men needing less fat than women. The critical fat for a man is 4%, while it is 11% for women. That means that the average person should not measure below those levels. Male athletes will typically range between 4% and 12% fat, whereas female athletes will normally fall in the 11–18% range. Normal levels for average, college-age males are 12–18%, with females normally ranging from 16% to 24%. Ranges above those normal ranges indicate that lowering body composition should be considered a priority.

Acknowledging that BIA scales vary in validity and reliability, one should not get overly caught up in the ranges presented above. Instead, it is more important to get a baseline reading and then compare all future measures back to the baseline. Of course, it is critical to maintain as much consistency as possible in taking the measurements, meaning that one should test at the same time of day, in the same clothing, and following the same testing requirements as described earlier. If the testing procedures are similar, the main emphasis should be placed on the body fat percentage dropping, regardless of the numbers.

Flexibility

Flexibility is perhaps the most underrated component of fitness in the United States. Most people put great effort into making time for cardiovascular training and strength training, yet a considerably lesser number of people will do the same for flexibility. When you consider the importance of flexibility, the disproportion is inexcusable. Muscle and joint flexibility promotes good posture, reduces the risk of musculoskeletal injuries, improves circulation, and produces a sense of calm in one's body. Without regular flexibility training, all of those qualities decrease. Far too often, people become incapacitated by lower back pain and injuries, most of which were preventable. The key to that prevention, and well as the rehabilitation, is flexibility training.

The most popular method of measuring flexibility is to measure the flexibility of the lower back and hamstrings with a sit-and-reach box. However, most do not have access to a sit-and-reach box,

> ——— **Tip 3.1** ———
>
> Flexibility training is often neglected, but it is one of the easiest components of fitness to improve. Flexibility also plays a substantial role in maintaining the body's ability to perform in muscular and cardiovascular activities.

so an appropriate substitution can be had by taping a tape measure or yardstick to the floor. After securing the yardstick or tape measure to the floor, place a line of tape at the 15 inch mark, and that will serve as the anchor for one's feet. The procedures for the sit-and-reach are as follow:

- Barefooted, place the feet on the tape at the 15 inch mark;
- Take a deep breath in while raising the hands above the head (or just outstretched in front of the body), interlocking the fingers;
- Keeping the legs straight, fully exhale while bending forward, reaching up the tape measure, without bouncing. Note: either a partner should read and record the measurement or stick a piece of tape down on the measuring device;
- Go back to the starting position;
- Take a total of three trials, with the furthest reach being the recorded score.

Generally speaking, women should score higher on the sit-and-reach than men, and the young should slightly outperform those who are older. Average men should be able to reach between 15 and 22 inches, and any score above 22 inches is excellent. Scores below 15 inches indicate a need to improve flexibility. Women with average flexibility will fall between 18 and 24 inches, with any score above 24 inches being excellent. Scores below 15 inches indicate a need to improve flexibility. Those who need to improve flexibility should be referring to Chapter Four to develop a protocol for regular flexibility training.

Muscular Strength

Muscular strength is one's ability to move an object. The standard test for muscular strength is to perform a one-rep maximum (1 RM) of an exercise that involves the target muscle as a prime mover (e.g. the bench press for the chest or the squat for the quadriceps and gluteal muscles). That means that the exerciser lifts as much weight as he or she possibly can while completing one repetition. A 1-RM test is dangerous and requires proper spotting from capable spotters.

A more appropriate test of muscular strength, for a single person to perform, is the chin-up test. However, because many people cannot perform a single chin-up, the test will not yield overwhelming results. Therefore, an appropriate compromise is the flexed arm hang, which has an element of muscular endurance to it as well. The procedures for the flexed arm hang are as follow:

- Use a horizontal bar (a well-mounted door jamb or beam can also be used), position a clock where it can be observed from a position just above the bar;
- Place a chair or sturdy wooden box on the floor beneath the bar;
- Step onto the box, putting both hands on the bar, palms facing away from the body, in line with the elbows when the upper arms are parallel to the ground;
- If the chin is not already above the bar, jump up until the chin is above the bar, and maintain a hanging position;

Figure 3.2 The flexed arm hang is a test that can be performed just about anywhere and by anyone. To earn an average score on the flexed arm hang, a lot of muscle and determination will be required.

- Begin recording the hanging time using the clock from the first bullet or count the seconds in the head (One-Mississippi, Two-Mississippi, etc.);
- Bend the knees slightly to ensure that no contact will be made with the chair or box;
- Hold the body still, with the chin above the bar, for as long as possible;
- Once the chin dips below the bar, the test is over;
- Record the total number of seconds hung.

Generally speaking, men should be able to hang longer than women on this test. Men should be able to hang for a minimum of 15 seconds, while 8 seconds is a good score for women. Those who hang for less than the desired times should look to improve muscular strength by following the information presented in Chapter Six.

Muscular Power

Muscular power measures one's ability to do more work in a shorter period of time. In essence, muscular power is what makes fast people fast and slow people slow. Muscular power is the attribute that gives some people the ability to jump high. In other words, muscular power is that attribute that differentiates the truly gifted anaerobic sports' athletes from lesser athletes.

The best indication of one's muscular power is the vertical jump. There are many variations of the vertical jump protocol, with the three most popular being a run-in, two-footed jump, a run-in, one-footed jump, or a step-in, two-footed jump. The purest test is the step-in, two-footed jump test, which minimizes momentum. The procedures for the step-in, two-footed jump test are as follow:

- Tape a ruler to a wall or mark distances, by half inches, up a wall. Be sure that the wall is empty and there is at least five feet of clear floor space at that part of the wall;
- After warming up well, stand with both feet on the floor, standing tall, and reach the inside arm up the ruler as far as possible;
- A partner should read the measurement of the initial reach up the wall, or if there is no partner, mark the spot by sticking a piece of tape to that height;
- Bring the outstretched arm back down;

- Step back with one foot, rocking is allowed;
- In one motion, step forward again and jump off both feet. Note: Use the entire body to explode up as high as possible. The knees should bend, the arms swing back, and then everything should project vertically at takeoff;
- The same arm that was used in the pre-jump measurement should reach up the ruler and tap the ruler, again using a partner or tape to identify the peak jump height;
- Three total jumps should be performed, with about a minute's rest between jumps;
- The highest jump height should be used. To get the vertical jump distance, the initial reach height should be subtracted from the highest vertical jump height.

Generally speaking, men should jump higher than women. Men who score a jump of 21.25 inches or more demonstrate excellent muscular power, while the average male should be able to jump a minimum of 15.75 inches. Women who can jump 17.25 inches demonstrate excellent muscular power, while the average woman should be able to jump a minimum of 10.5 inches. Those who desire to improve their muscular power would be best served by working with plyometric exercises two times a week, for two-week cycles broken up by one week of rest (see Chapter Six).

Muscular Endurance

Muscular endurance is one's ability to repeat a muscular activity over a long period of time. Muscular endurance testing is the easiest to perform, and there are numerous tests to test the endurance of just about any muscle grouping in the body. The two most popular tests are the push-up test and the sit-up test. Because they both test important muscle groups, both tests are detailed in this section.

The push-up test is used to evaluate upper body muscular endurance, more specifically, those muscles of the chest and triceps. The push-up test requires men to perform a full-body push-up, while women perform modified push-ups. The exerciser bends the elbows to 90° and then returns to the up position (for a more in-depth description of the proper push-up, please see Chapter Six). The exerciser goes until exhaustion, without taking any rest during the test. The number of successful push-ups performed is the score.

© Shutterstock/George Dolgikh

© Shutterstock/antoniodiaz

Figure 3.3 Women may either do modified (left) or full (right) push-ups for a push-up test. Meeting the norms while doing full push-ups only signifies even greater muscular strength and endurance.

To receive an excellent rating, men in their 20s should perform more than 40 push-ups, men in their 30s should perform 30, and men in their 40s and over should perform over 25 or more. Men who score fewer than 25, 20, and 15 push-ups, respectively, need to work on their muscular endurance. Women who score 30, 27, and 25 push-ups, respective to the aforementioned age groups, have excellent muscular endurance. Scoring fewer than 20, 17, and 15 push-ups, per the respective age groups, is an indication that greater emphasis needs to be put into muscular endurance training.

The sit-up test requires the exerciser to perform as many sit-ups as possible in one minute. In performing the sit-up: the exerciser's feet should be held down by a partner or secured under a fixed support; the exerciser's arms should be across the chest with the hands on the opposite shoulders; the exerciser should sit up until the elbows touch the thighs; and the exerciser returns to the ground and repeats. The number of complete sit-ups is counted as the final score.

The average sit-up test score for men is 30, while an excellent score is 45 sit-ups or more. Scoring below 30 sit-ups is an indication that additional abdominal work is need. For women, scores of 25 and 40 rank as average and excellent, respectively. Women who complete fewer than 25 sit-ups should work to improve their abdominal endurance.

Aerobic Power

Aerobic power, also known as VO_{2max}, is often thought to be the same thing as cardiovascular endurance. However, while VO_{2max} is the maximum amount of oxygen one's body can take in, distribute, and use, additional variables, such as anaerobic threshold and economy, play into endurance. Aerobic power is a better indicator of a person's top capacity for doing aerobic work (what is the fastest one can go and still be aerobic).

Testing for aerobic power can be quite intense, and in a lab setting, it often is. High-performance athletes, or those who are dealing with cardiovascular health issues, often undergo rigorous testing known as a maximal graded exercise test (GXT). A maximal GXT requires the exerciser to exercise until complete exhaustion or until other physiological markers are achieved. There is an extensive amount of high-tech, expensive equipment required for such a test. A less strenuous, submaximal GXT is easier on those being tested, and it requires minimal equipment. In theory, a person could

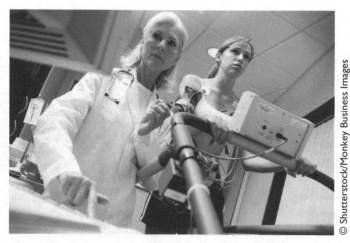

© Shutterstock/Monkey Business Images

Figure 3.4 Maximal GXT requires monitoring the heart's activity with an EKG machine and collection of gasses, inhaled and exhaled, using a metabolic cart and face mask (not pictured).

perform a submaximal GXT on a measured course, but it is best performed on a treadmill and with the use of a heart rate monitor. For some, the most difficult part of the test is doing the math required to determine VO_{2max}.

About Aerobic Power

Sandy is a twenty-eight-year-old woman who is looking to improve her cardiovascular fitness. The fitness floor attendant at her local fitness center put Sandy through a GXT to determine her VO_{2max}. Sandy was hoping that she would have a relative VO_{2max} of 35 ml O2 · kg⁻l · min⁻l. Her data and graph are below.

Age predicted maximum heart rate = 220–age = 220–28 = 192

Stage 1: 3.5 mph, 0% grade with a VO_2 of 12.88 ml $O_2 \cdot kg^{-1} \cdot min^{-1}$, heart rate = 104 bpm

Stage 2: 3.5 mph, 3% grade with a VO_2 of 15.41 ml $O_2 \cdot kg^{-1} \cdot min^{-1}$, heart rate = 122 bpm

Stage 3: 3.5 mph, 6% grade with a VO_2 of 17.95 ml $O_2 \cdot kg^{-1} \cdot min^{-1}$, heart rate = 141 bpm

Stage 4: 3.5 mph, 9% grade with a VO_2 of 20.48 ml $O_2 \cdot kg^{-1} \cdot min^{-1}$, heart rate = 152 bpm

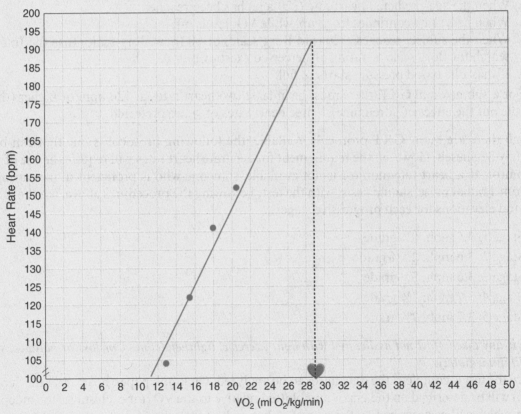

Sandy's Aerobic Power

Sandy's VO_{2max} is estimated at 29 ml $O_2 \cdot$ kg⁻l $\cdot$ min⁻l

There are many protocols one could follow to conduct a submaximal GXT. As well, a submaximal GXT can be performed on any cardiovascular machine (e.g. treadmill, bicycle, and upper body ergometer). The following procedures are for performing a GXT on a treadmill:

- Dress in comfortable, loose-fitting clothing and running shoes;
- Wear a heart rate monitor (there should be a bigger piece that straps on around the chest and a watch monitor);
- Be sure that the heart rate monitor is working properly;
- Start the treadmill belt with each foot on one side of the treadmill deck, straddling the treadmill belt until the belt gets moving;
- Track the belt with one foot (let the foot move along on top of the belt, gliding slowly back with the belt) until comfortable, and then begin walking;
- Without holding on, walk at the beginning pace and elevation for three minutes;
- At the 0:45 mark, record the heart rate; record it again at 1:45 and 2:30;
- The 1:45 and 2:30 heart rates should be within five bpm of each other;
- If the two heart rates are within five beats of one another, the 2:30 heart rate should be recorded, and the exercise should progress to the next stage. If the heart rates are not within five bpm, the exerciser should stay at the same pace for another minute, recording a 3:30 heart rate and aiming for the five bpm difference between the 2:30 and 3:30 heart rates;
- A maximal GXT is terminated when:
  - The subject has expressed that he or she cannot do any more (volitional fatigue);
  - When the age-predicted heart rate (220-age) has been reached;
  - When heart rate continues to go up, while VO_2 levels off;
  - When the subject reaches a 20 (old Borg scale) or 10 (new Borg scale) (use the Internet to search for Borg scale or rating of perceived exertion);
  - If diastolic blood pressure starts to fall.
- For a submaximal GXT, there must be at least two heart rates at 120 bpm or higher (this is to rule out the effect of adrenaline). Three heart rates of $\geq$ are preferred.

Although there are many GXT protocols available, the following protocol is one that can be done completely be oneself. However, the requirement for accurate heart rates will require the use of a heart rate monitor. If a heart rate monitor is not available, someone who is proficient in measuring heart rates, from a radial pulse, should assist with the test. Following the procedures above, use the following speeds and elevations for each progressive stage:

- Stage 1: 3.5 mph, 0% grade
- Stage 2: 3.6 mph, 2.5% grade
- Stage 3: 3.6 mph, 5% grade
- Stage 4: 3.7 mph: 7% grade
- Stage 5: 3.7 mph, 9% grade

If there is any discomfort not associated with light exercise, lightheadedness, or loss of balance, stop the treadmill immediately.

Once the test is complete, the data needs to be analyzed. On graph paper, heart rate (the dependent variable) will be described on the y-axis and plotted relative to the VO_2 for each stage (the independent variable, which will be described on the x-axis). A line of best fit will be drawn up to the horizontal line denoting the estimated maximum heart rate, and a vertical line will be drawn from that intersection down to the x-axis. The intersection of the x-axis is the estimate of VO_{2max}. This graphing technique is demonstrated in "About Aerobic Power."

In order to determine VO_2 for each stage, the following equations must be used:

$$VO_2 = VO_{2horizontal} + VO_{2vertical}$$
$$VO_{2horizontal} = \text{speed (in mph)} \cdot 26.8 \cdot 0.1 + 3.5$$
$$VO_{2vertical} = \text{speed (in mph)} \cdot 26.8 \cdot \text{grade (expressed as a decimal)} \cdot 0.9$$

Using those equations, the calculation of walking at 3.5 mph up a 7% grade would look like this:

$$VO_2 = VO_{2horizontal} + VO_{2vertical}$$
$$VO_{2horizontal} = 3.5 \cdot 26.8 \cdot 0.1 + 3.5 = 93.8 \cdot 0.1 + 3.5 = 9.38 + 3.5 = \mathbf{12.88}$$
$$VO_{2vertical} = 3.5 \cdot 26.8 \cdot 0.07 \cdot 0.9 = 93.8 \cdot 0.07 \cdot 0.9 = 6.566 \cdot 0.9 = \mathbf{5.9094}$$
$$VO_2 = VO_{2horizontal} + VO_{2vertical} = 12.88 + 5.9094 = 18.7894 \text{ or } \mathbf{17.79 \ ml \ O2 \cdot kg^{-1} \cdot min^{-1}}$$

These VO_{2max} are relative values, wherein the units associated with the VO_{2max} are ml $O_2 \cdot kg^{-1} \cdot min^{-1}$, which is read as milliliters of oxygen per kilogram of body weight per minute of exercise. Absolute VO_2 ignores the person's body weight. Men will have greater absolute VO_{2max} values than women. However, in relative terms, a well-trained woman could easily have a higher relative VO_{2max} than an untrained male.

With respect to relative VO_{2max}, average men should be in the high thirties range (35–39 ml $O_2 \cdot kg^{-1} \cdot min^{-1}$), while women should be in the low thirties range (30–35 ml $O_2 \cdot kg^{-1} \cdot min^{-1}$). Members of either sex would be very strong with VO_{2max} values greater than 50 ml $O_2 \cdot kg^{-1} \cdot min^{-1}$.

Conclusion

Physical fitness relies on a variety of physiological components working in concert. While many people will focus on only a couple of the components, all of the components are complimentary, and it is prudent to spend some time training each component each and every week. Using the tests contained in this chapter will help the reader establish goals for improving each component of fitness. As well, the tests should be conducted regularly in order to determine what progress is being made in each component.

Tip 3.2

The VO_2 equation for walking in only valid for speeds up to 3.7 mph. Once the walking speeds exceed 3.7 mph, the equation becomes less accurate in predicting actual oxygen uptake.

In Practice

Quantifying your physical fitness can help you understand where you are as well as where you need to go. Complete the table below by listing:

- Your scores for each test (for the VO_{2max}, include a graph that shows how you came to your score, as well as the math work for your equations);
- Your fitness norms category (use a search engine to find a norm chart for each variable and enter the classification [poor, average, excellent, etc.]);
- And your appraisal of where you are and how you should look to change.

Fitness Component	Score	Rank	Your Appraisal
Body Composition			
Flexibility			
Muscular Strength			
Muscular Power			
Muscular Endurance			
Aerobic Power			

WARM-UP, STRETCHING, AND COOL DOWN

Introduction

To many, the actual workout is not only the main focus of an exercise session, but the only focus. Too often, an exerciser will either fail to allot time for a warm-up and cool down, or the benefit of warming up and cooling down is under appreciated. By preparing the body for exercise, warm-up improves performance and reduces the risk of injury. Additionally, a cool down allows the body to recover naturally, which reduces the negative effects of a workout and speeds the recovery process. This chapter discusses the physiology of warming up and cooling down, including the appropriate inclusion of stretching.

The Physiology of Warm-Up

Heading out the door, sneakers on and ready to walk, Angie begins walking at her usual 4.5 mph pace. Today, however, is a little different. Angie left her headphones at home, hoping to take in a bit more of what nature has to offer. Without the headphones, Angie has a keener awareness of what is going on around her, yet it is not the chirping birds, the rustling of the wind-swept leaves, or the sound of traffic that has gained her attention. No, it's her breathing. It's rapid, slightly labored, and a lot louder than she ever imagined. Angie notices something else; today's walk *feels* harder than the normal routine. She checks her GPS watch, and she verifies that her speed is appropriate. Angie's not sick, and she got enough sleep last night. What is going on?

The truth be told, Angie probably isn't working any harder today than any other day; she is probably not breathing any faster, harder, or louder than ever. Without the distraction of her music, she just happens to be more observant of the physiology that accompanies oxygen deficit. To a degree, beginning any exercise bout will elicit an oxygen deficit. Oxygen deficit occurs when one begins exercising at an intensity that demands more oxygen than one can immediately take in. When a person goes from sitting down or standing passively to exercise at intensity, he or she is going from a very low need for oxygen to a substantially higher need. For example, when going from sitting in a chair to walking at 4.5 mph, the oxygen requirements increase approximately 454%.

The rapid and hard breathing experienced at the beginning of a walking session is the body's attempt to meet that greater oxygen need as quickly as possible. This period of increased oxygen uptake is referred to as the rapid VO_2 component of exercise. The greater the deficit and the longer it takes to get to homeostasis (the point where the oxygen need and oxygen uptake are equal), the more lactic acid your body will produce. It is a common belief that lactic acid is the enemy, although discussions later in this chapter will shed some light on the accuracy of that belief. Lactic acid is the waste product of anaerobic exercise, but real trouble begins only when the concentration of lactic acid in the

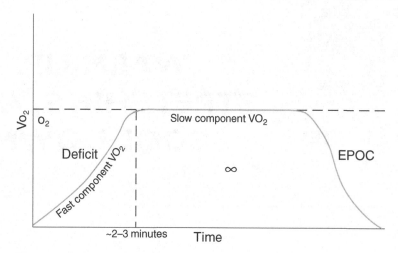

Figure 4.1 The author's rendition of the VO₂ curve.

blood starts to accumulate exponentially (1 molecule begets 2 molecules, which beget 4 more, then 16 more, etc.). When lactic acid accumulates, muscles fatigue, and when muscles fatigue, workouts end prematurely. Luckily, most people achieve homeostasis within two to three minutes of establishing a consistent workout intensity. Instead of remaining in anaerobic metabolism, the body converts to the much more efficient aerobic energy system, as represented by the relatively flat line in Figure 4.1. This stage of metabolism is the slow component VO₂.

Warming up is the key to experiencing a less intense oxygen deficit, thus limiting the physiological and psychological stresses of acute exercise. Warm-up can be very time consuming or quite short, with the length of time most heavily dependent upon the intensity of the intended workout. Therefore, most walking workouts require a fairly short warm-up session. A walking warm-up should start with low-intensity movements followed by a progressively more intense demand, up to walking intensity. For example, a person who wants to go for a fitness-oriented walk might stand up, perform some light leg swings (with control, swinging the leg backward and forward, then side-to-side, progressively making the swings a bit larger each time), perform a few lunges, and then head out the door with a slightly less intense pace for the first minute or two, ramping up to the intended walking pace. Someone going out for a casual walk could forego all of the other steps and simply head out the door at a slower pace than goal, progressively increasing intensity over the first four to six minutes until a desired pace is achieved. In contrast to those conditions, a race walker might warm up for 45 minutes, bringing in a combination of stretching, low and higher intensity movements, and strides (short [~100 meters] repetitions) at the desired race pace.

In addition to allowing the body to slowly adapt to the increased demand for oxygen, warm-up decreases the risk of injury. By slowly increasing the demand on the body, warm-up provides one's muscles the ability to increase temperature, mobility, and blood flow. Warmer, more pliable muscles are much more resistant to strains (tears) and cramps. Warm-up is most essential in the prevention of shin splints and plantar fascia, two of the most debilitating injuries known to walkers. In addition to helping to prevent injuries, warmer muscles work more efficiently, leading to increased performance and a more valuable workout.

Warming up the body prior to a fitness walk is essential to bringing about increased performance, injury prevention, and the decrease in metabolic byproducts. A sufficient warm-up will increase heart rate to a level closer to that needed to maintain the expected performance goal, increase respiration rate and depth, and increase muscle temperature and flexibility. For lower intensity walks, simply slowing increase speed to the desired pace may be enough, but for sessions that will require higher intensities, a more progressive warm-up that includes dynamic range of motion exercises will be required.

A Progressive Warm-Up

A progressive warm-up is essential to increase muscle temperature, respiration rate, and heart rate, thereby preparing your body for more intense exercise and lessening the harmful waste products that develop from starting your workout with a large oxygen deficit. This sample warm-up could be done in approximately 10 minutes and would be suitable for a moderately high-intensity walk.

Walk and stretch (walk three steps; lift the toe of the front foot; reach down to smoothly touch the raised toe with the hand on the same side of the body; hold for one second; repeat by alternating sides for a total of 30–40 repetitions of the stretch).

High-step walks (walk 30–40 steps with each step lifting the knee as high as possible [toward the chest] before completing the step).

Soldier walks (walk 30–40 steps with each step lifting the leg up in front of the body, from the hip, keeping the knee straight, prior to completing the step).

Skips and arm swings (perform a low-legged skip while swinging the arms about the shoulders; 20–30 skips with arms swinging forward, 20–30 skips with arms swinging backward).

Walk with knee pulls (walk three steps; stop; pull the front leg up, with your arms, so that the knee comes up to the chest [stretching buttocks]; three steps alternate pull; repeat for 20–30 pulls).

Lunge walks (walk three steps; lunge forward into the front leg, making the back leg straight; hold for two seconds; repeat alternating legs for 20–30 stretches).

Leg swings (15 side-to-side leg swings, about the hip, in front of the anchored leg; switch legs; switch legs to go 15 front-to-back with the original leg; switch).

Types of Stretching Protocols

At any athletic event or fitness facility, individuals can be seen preparing for physical activity by stretching, yet there is usually considerable variation in the types of stretching being done. The different stretching protocols have arisen from the different application physiological concepts, with the main concepts being relaxation, over-compensation, and reciprocal inhibition. This section will explain the physiological properties that allow for increased flexibility through stretching training.

The most popular standard form of stretching is generally classified as static stretching. Static stretching relies on the relaxation of the agonist (target) muscle. Further, static stretching involves moving a joint into a position that pulls the agonist muscle into its greatest length. For example, to stretch the quadriceps muscles (front of the thigh), one would pull his or her heel to his or her buttocks, bending the knee as much as possible, while keeping the hip straight. Static stretching relies on the muscle's willingness to relax in order to make that stretch possible, and the longer the stretch is held, the more relaxed the agonist becomes. Static stretches should be held for at least 30 seconds, and they can be held for extended periods of time, even for several minutes. Muscles that are larger and cross over more than one joint should be held for longer periods of time than smaller muscles. Daily static stretching of the body's large muscle groups can alleviate joint pain and reduce tension.

© Shutterstock/barang

Figure 4.2 Static stretching is used to provide a more relaxing and long-term stretching of the muscles. Therefore, static stretches are held for long periods of time (often minutes) and should be performed when the muscles are warm, preferably after the workout. Performing static stretches prior to exercise signals muscles to relax rather than being ready for action.

Another popular form of stretching is proprioceptive neuromuscular facilitation (PNF) stretching, which is a very scientific way of saying that one is contracting and relaxing his or her muscles to elicit a greater stretch than can normally be achieved through static stretching. The drawback to PNF stretching is that it requires a partner or the well-practiced use of a rope or yoga strap, which makes it a more challenging task than static stretching. In order to gain the benefits from PNF stretching, one has to manipulate the overcompensating relaxation that follows an intense contraction. The concept in play is that an intense contraction generates a lot of neurological feedback, to which the brain responds with an exaggerated relaxation. Pulling or pushing the agonist deeper into stretch, while the overcompensation is still occurring, allows the limb to move past the point at which it was limited in the last stretch sequence.

If a client is looking to PNF stretch his or her quadriceps muscles, he or she lies on his or her stomach, at which point the stretching technician pushes the client's heel toward the buttocks, holding that stretch for a few seconds. Releasing that hold slightly, the technician asks the subject to try to extend his or her leg, as the technician pushes against the leg to keep the knee from extending. After a few seconds, the technician instructs the client to relax, and as he or she does, the technician pushes the heel closer to the buttocks, thereby stretching the quadriceps even further. This sequence is repeated up to six times. For even greater flexibility gains, the technician pushes the heel down with his or her shoulder while lifting the client's knee off the ground an inch or two with his or her forehand (that which is on the outside of the leg that is being stretched). By pulling the thigh off the ground, the technician is also extending the quadriceps muscles at the point of origin (at the hip).

As can be ascertained, PNF stretching is a more aggressive mode of stretching that can produce substantial increases in muscle temperature. It also increases (facilitates) neuromuscular function (nerves fire to produce muscular contraction) and proprioception (awareness of relationship in space), thereby awakening the muscles and preparing them for action. These attributes will come into further perspective later on in this chapter.

> ## Tip 4.1
>
> Although not discussed in this chapter, yoga is a terrific way to increase flexibility, as it provides long-term flexibility and develops core strength, balance, and greater proprioception.

Another active form of stretching, introduced by Jim and Phil Wharton, is aptly named Active Isolated (AI) stretching. While PNF relies on contraction and relaxation of the agonist muscle, AI stretching relies on the principle of reciprocal inhibition. Reciprocal inhibition is the act of one muscle relaxing while it's antagonist is contracting. For example, if one wants to maximize the efforts of the biceps, the triceps muscles must relax, eliminating any resistance the triceps muscles might offer the biceps group. Like PNF, AI stretching also requires a partner or rope, but its methodology makes the individual performance of the stretches much more manageable.

For simplicity, let's look at stretching the hamstring group as an example. The client who wants to stretch his or her hamstrings lies down on his or her back, with the target leg out straight and the other leg bent, with the bottom of the foot flat to the floor. Wrapping the rope around the ball of the foot on the target side, the client contracts his or her quadriceps muscles, pulling his or her leg as far up as he or she can with the muscles alone. As the client reaches the limit established by his or her muscles, he or she uses the rope to gently pull the leg further back over his or her head. The pull should only last approximately two seconds. Using his or her quadriceps to eccentrically lower his or her leg back toward the floor, he or she contracts the quadriceps again, just before his or her heel touches, bringing the leg back up and starting the stretch process again. It is essential that the movements are smooth, controlled, and fluid. All of the actions are controlled by the antagonist, which, in this case, was the quadriceps group. A set of six to ten stretches is usually appropriate for AI stretching.

The final stretch protocol is the most controversial. Ballistic stretching is exactly what the name implies, having to do with the flight or movement of a projectile against gravity. One example of a ballistic exercise is the act of jumping up into the air, pulling one's legs to his or her chest, and then landing back on the ground due to the failure to escape gravity's pull. Another example of ballistic

© Shutterstock/adamgregor

Figure 4.3 A well-trained partner can provide both PNF and AI stretching to help one prepare for a competition or workout.

© Shutterstock/Maridav

Figure 4.4 Although controversial, ballistic movements stretch the body and prepare it for the dynamic stretch-shortening cycle that will ensue once a workout or competition begins.

exercise is running, which, as is discussed in Chapter Five, is mechanically different from walking in very important ways. A third example was presented earlier in this chapter, the suggestion of using a leg swing within the warm-up. In a leg swing, the leg swings like a pendulum, rotating about the hip. However, the motion is limited by the quadriceps, when traversing backward, and by the hamstrings, when traversing forward. As the leg swings down from the established limits, gravity accelerates the leg, providing momentum that is able to subtly overcome the limits of the acting muscle, thereby bringing about the most incremental increase in flexibility with each successive swing.

Those who argue against ballistic stretching suggest that the acceleration and deceleration of the body puts extensive stress on the axis point and the muscles attached. There is concern that such stresses will lead to a muscle strain, ligament sprain, or avulsion fracture. They further support their argument that the somewhat limited gains do not project enough benefit to overcome the risks. Proponents of ballistic stretching argue that many athletic movements are ballistic in nature, and the best way to prepare for intense action is to produce lesser actions (ballistic stretches) that excite and prepare the muscles and joints for the tasks at hand.

As presented, there are a variety of stretching options, and each individual will likely formulate an opinion as to which works best. The next section discusses where each method of stretching is best employed to enhance flexibility and performance while helping to prevent injuries.

When to Stretch

Flexibility is critical to human performance as well as lessening joint and muscular pain. While just about any type of stretching can produce the latter of those outcomes, increasing performance requires the right stretching at the right time. This section reviews the most appropriate times to employ each stretching protocol.

As one should recall, warm-up is a progression of activities that increase heart rate, respiration rate, muscle temperature, and more. It's also important to remember that muscles are more flexible when they are warm. Therefore, stretching one's muscles should only be done after they have been warmed up a little.

A good way to start a warm-up is with some very low-level ambulation (mainly walking) for about three to five minutes. As discussed earlier, even this walking should begin at a light intensity that increases with each minute. After heart rate and body temperature are somewhat increased, it is appropriate to begin stretching; however, for lower intensity sessions, it may also be suitable to start right into the walking session. At this stage of the warm-up, it is most appropriate to perform either PNF or AI stretching, as both actively involve muscles in the stretching process, and they can help to maintain the slightly elevated heart rate that is preferable in warm-up. At this point, ballistic stretching is generally not advisable, although a low-intensity ballistic stretch (e.g. leg swings) would be appropriate. High-intensity ballistic movements are better saved for later in the warm-up sequence, as the body is not physiologically prepared enough for high-intensity ballistic stretches (like jumping with knee tucks). Static stretching is not recommended in the warm-up sequence at all. As you recall, static stretching relies on the muscles relaxing and becoming calm, which is in direct contrast to the objectives established for warm-up.

After completing the PNF or AI stretching sequence, the warm-up process should continue by shifting back to ambulatory movements. Again, if the target pace is of low enough intensity, this may be the time to actually start walking, starting slightly slower than goal pace, but at a pace that can be much faster than if no warm-up was performed at all. For higher intensity walking sessions, the goal of this stage of the warm-up is to increase heart rate and temperature closer to that required for the actual workout session. Implementing strides will prepare the body to go at full goal pace. To perform a stride, simply select a short distance (roughly 100 meters) and divide that distance into thirds. The first third of the stride should be performed at a comfortable walking pace, while the second third should get to a comfortably hard pace, and the final third hard. Five to six of these strides will allow bring one's heart rate and muscular readiness to a level commensurate with the desired workout pace. At this time, should there be any need for additional mobility, this stage of the warm-up is appropriate for adding some ballistic movements. A few knee tucks, some soldier kicks (trying to bring the toes up to the hands held out in front of the body at shoulder height), or even one-legged hops with cycle (see Chapter Six) are all appropriate to increase one's physiological preparedness a little more.

As important as warm-up is, cool down is of equal or greater value. The amount of time spent cooling down should be proportionate with the intensity of the workout, for the reasons specified in the next section of this chapter. It is the cool down phase of the workout where static stretching plays a considerable role.

Remember that static stretching is a held stretch that can last for minutes at a time and which signals the muscles to relax and rest. The two main objectives of static stretching are to elongate the muscle and to increase circulation to the muscle. Holding static stretches for extended time lengths forces the muscle to relax, and that relaxation sends signals to the nervous and endocrine systems that it is time to decrease the neural and hormonal stimulants for exercise intensity. As well, the increased lengthening of the muscle allows for greater circulation, thereby allowing for the removal of wastes and the replenishing of carbohydrates and proteins, at the cellular level.

When performing static stretching, patience is key. The muscle should move into the stretch position and be applied with just enough force to feel a very light tension in the muscle. The motion should be very deliberate, taking the agonist into stretch until the tension develops. As the stretch is being held, the tension will lessen or go away completely. At that point, the stretch should be increased in order to maintain the light tension. Continuously increase the stretch until the desired goal time for the stretch is achieved. Depending on one's long-term flexibility goals, static stretching sessions should last a half hour or longer. However, most people can achieve positive, long-term results by stretching 15 minutes a day.

The Benefits of Cool Down

Physiologically speaking, cool down is even more important than warm-up. Cool down allows the body's systems to slowly return to homeostasis and decreases the time needed to recover from a workout. Cool down lessens potential discomfort, resulting from the strain of the workout, and makes the next workout even better.

© Shutterstock/warrengoldswain

Figure 4.5 Don't just stand there! Even though a workout may have led to exhaustion, a cool down involving low-intensity exercise and static stretching will improve recovery by decreasing lactic acid, bringing heart rate and respiration rate down more efficiently, and providing stretch training to the muscles.

As can be observed in Figure 4.1, once activity is stopped, there is a rapid decrease in the oxygen required to meet the body's metabolic demands; however, the exerciser's respiration rate remains high. This is known as excessive post-oxygen consumption (EPOC), and it is relative to the oxygen deficit and intensity of the workout. The main function of EPOC is to provide oxygen that can be used to buffer the lactic acid produced during the workout.

It was previously stated that lactic acid is the metabolic waste product of anaerobic (without oxygen) metabolism. Even when homeostasis is achieved, during a workout, there is a small amount of anaerobic metabolism occurring. The higher the intensity is, the greater will be the anaerobic component, hence, the greater will be the lactic acid accumulation. Being an acid, lactic acid can throw off the delicate pH balance in the blood, leading to decreased physiological performance. However, by using oxygen, the body can break down lactic acid into hydrogen (which, when combined with oxygen provides the body with water) and lactate (buffering). Further breakdown of lactate results in pyruvate, which is used in the Krebs Cycle, providing the body with energy. Thus, by providing the body with oxygen, through EPOC, one converts potentially harmful lactic acid into beneficial products.

The buffering of lactic acid mainly occurs in the Type I muscle fibers. In order to maximize buffering, the Type I fibers need to remain metabolically active, but at a low enough intensity to break down the lactic acid without producing more. Therefore, a cool down should involve a slow walk of five to ten minutes. That walk should be slow enough to allow the heart rate to decrease to 100 bpm or less. Further, deep, controlled breathing should be employed in order to facilitate gas exchange in the lungs. Immediately following this walk, the cool down should transition into the 15 minutes, or longer, of static stretching as discussed earlier in this chapter.

In addition to allowing the body to buffer lactic acid, cool down increases the circulation of blood to the muscles. That increased circulation delivers both protein and carbohydrates to rebuild stores of glycogen and protein in the muscle cells (please see the recovery nutrition section of Chapter Eight). The increased circulation also delivers additional blood cells, namely platelets, to the muscle allowing the body to begin repairing any micro-tears that may have resulted from high-intensity work.

Conclusion

Warm-up and cool down are critically important to walking performance, musculoskeletal health, and recovery from workouts. It is important to devote as much time and energy to warming up and cooling down as to the actual workout time. As well, similar to other aspects of fitness, warming up and cooling down should be designed to meet the walker's individual needs and interests.

In Practice

On your next walk, take a watch with a second hand on it. Before walking, take your heart rate. Time the walk and make a note of the time at which you think that you reached steady state. At that moment, take your heart rate and record it. Note how long you remain in steady state, and as you stop your walk, take your pulse again (before you actually stop). Finally, at one minute after you stopped walking, take your heart rate again. Record how you felt. Complete the table below.

Variable	Data
Beginning HR	
Time to Steady State (min:sec)	
HR at the Beginning of Steady State	
HR at the End of Steady State	
Time in Steady State (min:sec)	
HR 1:00 Post-walk	
How Do You Feel at 1:00 Post-exercise	

MECHANICS OF WALKING

Introduction

Walking is the most common method of human locomotion between two points. Certainly, there are very different forms of walking, each with its purpose, but walking for fitness has two main forms, traditional fitness walking and race walking. While the mechanics of race walking will be discussed in brief, the emphasis of this chapter is to review the biomechanics of fitness walking itself and in comparison to running.

When it comes to discussing the biomechanics of any sport, one can spend a lot of time discussing various physics formulas and analyzing countless factors that can affect performance. Many do just that. However, the purpose of this chapter is to look at the biomechanics of walking in fairly simple terms, which will help the reader better understand the exercise, improve technique, reduce injury risk, and get the desired physiological benefit. This chapter specifically looks at the mechanics of a walking stride, with heavy emphasis on the mechanics of fitness walking. As well, the chapter will also compare the mechanics of walking and running and how the two forms of exercise can both complement and hinder one another.

Biomechanics of the Walking Stride

As alluded to in the introduction, biomechanics is a complicated science that studies the physics of human movement. Much of what is studied in biomechanics is centered around Newton's three laws of motion. Biomechanics emphasizes kinematics (simply defined as the mechanisms of angular motion, such as joint actions) and kinetics (simply defined as the forces and energy that effect motion). In order to explore the kinematic and kinetic properties of motion, biomechanists study angular motion, acceleration, levers, external forces, properties of motion, and much more. This particular section will look mostly at the kinematics of walking, particularly the joints in use, the angles at which those joints are employed, and adjustments that are made when the walking surface changes.

Leisure-paced and fitness walking both place heavy emphasis on the knee and ankle joints, while requiring much less activity in other joints. Race walking also stresses those joints, but the hip rotation is heavily emphasized as well. In race walking, the hips rotate to provide a greater swing of the leg to allow the foot to clear the ground more easily, thus increasing stride length. Therefore, while the fitness walking motion primarily occurs in the sagittal plane of motion, race walking occurs in the transverse, frontal, and sagittal planes. The extensive range of motion and dynamic muscular actions of race walking produce high degrees of joint friction and muscular soreness, making further discussion of the mechanics of race walking best reserved for conversations between the athlete and coach.

As previously stated, fitness walking mainly occurs in the sagittal plane, which divides the body in right and left halves, with the motions within the plane being flexion and extension (e.g. bending and straightening the knee or elbow, pointing the toes, or raising the arm in front of the body). Therefore, walking requires considerable flexion and extension of the hip and knee as well as plantar flexion and dorsiflexion of the ankle. As motion goes up the chain, from the ankle to the hip, the magnitude of the action, within each joint, decreases. As such, the ankle goes through the greatest percentage of its range of motion and the hip the least. The next few paragraphs will cover the actions occurring within each joint.

The actions at the ankle allow a walker to follow the natural walking pattern. The ankle inverts, a combination of dorsiflexion (toes pull up toward the knee) and supination (rolling toward the outside of the foot), in order to allow a walker's heel to make the initial contact with the ground. The greatest amount of impact occurs on the outside half of the heel. The calcaneus (heel bone) is the thickest of the bones of the feet, and it is protected by the heel pad. The heel pad is able to absorb and dissipate the force of the heel strike, while the calcaneus is able to resist the remaining pressure. Likewise, the direct alignment of the heel and tibia (the big bone in the shin) promotes transfer of additional force up the tibia for even greater dissipation of the impact forces.

Following initial impact, the force and energy that has not been dissipated is transferred across the foot. The transfer occurs diagonally, so that the weight is transferred to the big toe for push-off. The diagonal transfer of weight is the result of ankle eversion, which is the combination of pronation (rolling toward the big toe) and plantar flexion (toes pointing away from the body).

At push-off, plantar flexion is maximized, allowing for maximal plantar flexion of the foot/ankle. Plantar flexion creates a longer moment arm in the lower leg, which provides the force to propel the individual forward, demonstrating Newton's Third Law of Motion (every action creates an equal and opposite reaction). The push-off is well demonstrated in the left foot of the woman in Figure 5.1. One very important characteristic of walking is that there is always a foot in contact with the ground. While Figure 5.1 demonstrates the push-off phase in the left foot, the right leg is in a very strong position, where it will assume the support of the body in the stance phase.

Following the push-off, the leg goes into the swing phase. During the swing phase (see Figure 5.2), the hip goes from its farthest extension to its greatest flexion (back to front), while the knee is also

Figure 5.1 The left foot is demonstrating the push-off (or toe-off) while the right leg is grounded, demonstrating the stance phase.

© Shutterstock/lzf

Figure 5.2 The woman's right leg is in the swing phase, while the left leg is in the stance phase.

flexed. As a result, the leg swings from where the foot is well behind the body to where it is positioned underneath the torso. To finish the swing phase, the knee extends to almost 180°, in preparation for the landing phase. With the knee extended, the foot moves out in front of the body, and when combined with slight inversion of the foot and ankle, the walker is ready to make contact with the ground (see Figure 5.3). Upon impact, the foot roles through the steps described above, to complete the stance phase, and to prepare to push off once again. At the same time, the opposite foot has transitioned from push-off, into the swing phase, and is preparing for the landing phase.

While the joints provide the axes around which bones move, locomotion cannot occur without the actions of the muscles attached to those bones. Therefore, a review of the biomechanics of walking would not be complete without a discussion of the muscles used in each phase. The next few paragraphs will touch on the roles the muscles play in walking, and the next chapter is dedicated to training those muscles for increased strength and power.

Muscles can perform three actions as well as relaxing. It is important to understand each of those in order to appreciate the different roles the muscles will play throughout the walking stride. The first action a muscle can perform is a concentric contraction. By definition, a concentric contraction is the

Figure 5.3 The right leg of this walker demonstrates the landing phase where there is slight hip flexion, knee extension to 180°, and a heel strike on the outside (lateral) aspect of the heel. The left leg demonstrates the push-off phase where the hip is in neutral position, the knee is flexed to about 45°, and the foot is slightly everted to allow a push off the area of the big toe.

shortening of a muscle in order to bring about a decrease in joint angle. For example, the hamstring group contracts in order to flex (bend) the knee, thereby decreasing the interior (back) angle of the knee.

The second action a muscle can perform is the eccentric action. An eccentric action is defined as the forced lengthening of a muscle that brings about an increase in joint angle. Often, the eccentric action is called a negative. An example of the hamstring group being worked eccentrically is the straightening of the leg when performing a hamstring curl on a machine. To produce the forced lengthening, the resistance force must be greater than the muscular force. Therefore, in strength training, eccentric actions are often brought about by decreased neuromuscular stimulus that reduces the muscle involvement, thus allowing the resistance force to slowly extend the knee.

The third action a muscle can perform is a static contraction. A static contraction is an attempted shortening of the muscle that never comes about, as the muscular force is not enough to overcome the resistance applied by whatever the exerciser was trying to move. Static contractions are often used in order to provide support or stability to the body. Often, for example, the muscles of the core (abdominals, back extensors, hip flexors, and hip extensors) perform static contractions in order to stabilize and support the rest of the body.

Relaxation is the opposite of muscular action, whether that action is concentric, eccentric, or static. By definition, relaxation is the lack of muscular action brought about by no neuromuscular stimulus. The relaxation of a muscle tends to lead to an increase in joint angle, and so relaxation and eccentric action are often confused. Often, relaxation goes hand-in-hand with concentric contraction. When an agonist (working muscle) contracts, the antagonist (muscle on the opposite side of the joint) relaxes. For example, when the quadriceps group contracts to bring about knee extension, the hamstring group will relax in order to allow the extension to happen without resistance. The hamstring group's relaxation is more specifically termed reciprocal inhibition, as introduced in Chapter Four (not allowing action in the opposing muscle in order to permit the agonist's actions).

It is clear that the muscles of the leg take on various roles throughout the walking stride. Table 5.1 provides an overview of the major muscle groups and their actions during the walking stride.

Table 5.1 The Major Muscles of the Lower Body and Their Actions in Walking Stride.

Muscle/Muscle Group	Concentric Contractions	Eccentric Actions	Relaxation
Hip flexors (front of the hip)	Bringing the leg forward in the swing phase	Works eccentrically when the body moves forward through the stance phase Mild eccentric actions during push-off and landing phases	Rarely, if at all
Hip extensors (back of the hip [glutes])	Bringing the leg back (moving the body forward) during the stance phase Mild concentric contraction during the push-off phase	Works eccentrically during the landing phase	Rarely, if at all

Muscle/Muscle Group	Concentric Contractions	Eccentric Actions	Relaxation
Hip abductors (outside of hip and thigh) and hip adductors (inside of hip and thigh)	Rarely *note: these two muscle groups become much more engaged both concentrically and eccentrically during the race walking stride	Perform mild eccentric actions throughout the walking stride to provide stability to the upper leg	Rarely, if at all
Quadriceps group	Bringing about knee extension throughout the push-off and swing phases Assist in hip flexion in the swing phase	Heavy eccentric role in the landing phase that continues through the stance phase to maintain stability	Rarely, if at all One might think that the quadriceps would be relaxing through the stance phase, but a mild eccentric is needed to maintain knee integrity
Hamstring group	Bringing about knee flexion during the stance phase, although much of the knee flexion comes as a result of the foot being grounded and the body moving forward, so the eccentric action of the quadriceps group is of equal importance	Eccentric action during the landing phase to provide knee stability and prevent hyperextension Slight eccentric action to maintain knee flexion through the early swing phase	Rarely, if at all Like the quadriceps, hamstring actions are pretty relevant throughout the walking stride in order to maintain stability in the knee and hip
Calf (gastrocnemius, soleus, and Achilles tendon)	Major emphasis on concentric contraction in the push-off phase Increased concentric activity as the foot rolls through the stance phase Mild contraction to maintain plantar flexion during the early swing phase	Major emphasis on eccentric action during the landing phase Eccentric action continues through the early part of the stance phase	Relaxation occurs to allow the anterior tibialis to pull the foot into dorsiflexion at the end of the swing phase
Anterior tibialis (front of the shin)	Emphasis is on the later swing phase to pull the foot into dorsiflexion, preparing for landing	Heavy emphasis on the eccentric through the landing phase, tailing off slightly during the stance phase, and which progressively lightens throughout push-off and the first part of the swing phase	Rarely, if at all

Walking Versus Running

As previously mentioned in this chapter, the walking stride has a highly specific biomechanical component in that there must always be a foot in contact with the ground. At very fast paces, that principle puts tremendous rotational stress on the leg, which must be controlled, mainly, at the hip. For evidence of this, one needs to look no further than a race walking competition, particularly in the last mile of a longer competition, and especially when the racers cross the finish line. The agony on the faces of the racers may be enough to convince an observer to stay far away from the sport.

When one desires to improve fitness, one of the primary goals is to increase heart rate, thereby taxing the body more (see Chapter Seven). Logically, the faster one walks, the higher the heart rate response will be. However, given the stress that high-speed walking places on the hips, the desire for improved fitness may fall short of the discomfort that coincides. Therefore, an alternative to high-speed walking is desirable.

Biomechanically speaking, there is a more advantageous method of increasing heart rate through walking. Rather than emphasizing speed, one should consider increasing the incline. In fact, changes in incline have a more profound impact on intensity and heart rate response than does speed. For example, a person who normally walks at 3.5 mph and wants to increase intensity by 10% will need to walk at 3.85 mph. That is a change in pace from 17:08 per mile to 15:35 per mile, a difference of 1:33 per mile. To bring about the same increase in intensity through a change in elevation, the walker would be required to walk at 3.5 mph and a 0% grade to walking at 3.5 mph and a 1% grade, or going up one foot in elevation for every 100 feet of horizontal travel. As walking speeds increase, the effect of incline is even more profound.

Another benefit of emphasizing grade over speed is the change in mechanics that is required. While speed emphasizes stride length and increased stress on the hips (which will translate down to the knees and ankles), walking up hill actually puts greater emphasis on muscular action (hence the greater gains in heart rate). To walk up hill, there is an increased emphasis on push-off, leading to a greater vertical displacement of the knee. Therefore, the calf and quadriceps muscles must be more involved, leading to greater muscular strength and development. Additionally, stride length actually decreases some, leading to a decreased emphasis on hip rotation and greater stride frequency (leg turnover/quicker feet).

Despite the benefits of incline training, there are some barriers to employing it as well. First, incline training will require a hilly road or a treadmill. Not everyone has access to one or both of those. Second, by increasing the demand on the quadriceps and calf muscles, there will be a corresponding increase in muscular discomfort and fatigue as well as increased production of metabolic waste (lactic acid). Those barriers may lead some to remain committed to increased speed.

Chapter Seven is dedicated to different training methods to improve one's physical capacities. Additionally, Chapter Seven contains the argument that for high-end fitness, it is often better to introduce bouts of running into the weekly workout schedule. Simply, at fast speeds, the human body is more efficient running than it is walking. The rest of this section focuses on how running mechanics differ from walking mechanics and the physics-based rationale for considering running to supplement one's walking routine.

The greatest biomechanical difference between walking and running is the aspect of remaining grounded. Running features a flight phase, which means both feet are completely off the ground and the body is unsupported. Because of the need for the flight phase, there is a heavy emphasis on the push-off phase of the running stride. Contrary to the mild push-off and knee flexion that is used to cycle the walker's leg through the swing phase, the running push-off requires triple extension. The referenced triple extension refers to plantar flexion of the ankle, knee extension, and hip extension. The overwhelming muscular forces that produce that dynamic chain of joint actions allow the runner to overcome gravity, thereby taking flight.

Figure 5.4 Running differs from walking in that running features a flight stage that increases muscle involvement and stride length.

Yet another difference between the two activities is in the landing phase. While walkers land on their heels, running should emphasize a midfoot landing. Landing on one's heel, while running, provides a breaking mechanism that increases sheer on the tibia, eccentric actions of the quadriceps and calves, and causes a negative acceleration of the body (often commonly, mistakenly referred to as deceleration). Conversely, landing midfoot allows for an immediate transition to the push-off phase, leading to faster turnover, and more efficient running.

Rather than the extensive hip rotation that allows for increased stride length in very fast-paced walking, the increased stride length achieved in running is the result of the added vertical displacement allowing for increased horizontal travel. Because there is considerably less stress placed on the hips, running decreases the risk of joint injuries as compared to very fast-paced walking. Additionally, due

Figure 5.5 Fast runners land with a midfoot strike, rather than the heel strike of very slow runners and walkers. The midfoot strike allows for an immediate transition to the push-off phase, providing the runner with faster turnover and a more efficient stride.

to the increased stride length and short recovery period that comes from each flight phase, running is also more economical than high-speed walking. Finally, due to the gross muscular contractions that are used in running, runners are able to generate the higher heart rates that are needed to increase cardiovascular function, develop more muscle, and improve proprioception and neuromuscular function.

Despite the many positives that come from running training, there are potential drawbacks as well. Landing from the elevated position increases the eccentric load on the quadriceps and hamstring groups, the hip extensors (glutes), and both the anterior tibialis and the calf muscles (gastrocnemius, soleus, and Achilles tendon). Especially in novice runners, that added stress can lead to bone injuries (e.g. stress fractures or shin splints), extensive muscle soreness, and a faster rate of fatigue. Running also requires a faster turn-over of running gear, especially shoes, meaning it can be more expensive than walking.

Conclusion

Fitness walking is a low-impact activity that can be performed just about anywhere. The mechanical stress on the body's muscles and joints is minimal, making it the perfect exercise for novice fitness enthusiasts as well as those who are simply hoping to increase their activity levels some. For greater fitness improvement, to burn off more calories per minute, and to be able to increase strength, running is a terrific supplemental form of exercise. However, while running is more economical for moving at high speeds, there are drawbacks including muscular soreness, fatigue, and joint pain.

Walking mechanics will be influenced by speed and the grade of the ground on which one is walking. Moderate speed and moderate grade bring about the greatest overload in a walking workout, thereby increasing the heart's efficiency and strength. Ultimately, a variety of walking speeds, walking surfaces, and walking styles will provide the most diverse training, which is preferable for developing proprioception, muscular balance, and muscle tone.

In Practice

Take a field trip. Head to a local track, park, or fitness center and get to a place where you can observe walkers and runners. Pick four different people, one walking for leisure, one who is fitness walking, one who is jogging slowly, and one who is running quickly. Observe several strides (at least five or six steps, per leg, for each person). Answer the following questions regarding each person's gait.

Leisure walker

Describe the length of the walker's stride: _____

_____

_____

Describe the foot strike of this walker: _____

_____

_____

_____

Fitness walker

Describe the length of the walker's stride: _____

_____

_____

Describe the foot strike of this walker: _____

_____

_____

_____

Jogger

Describe the length of the jogger's stride: _____

_____

_____

Describe the foot strike of this jogger: _____

_____

_____

_____

Faster runner

Describe the length of the runner's stride: _____

_____

_____

_____

Describe the foot strike of this runner: _____

_____

_____

_____

_____

STRENGTH TRAINING FOR WALKERS

Introduction

A professor with a Ph.D. in exercise physiology, at a highly prestigious university, once made audacious advice that distance runners do not lift weights. That assumption could include walker as well. Others argue that walkers look to maintain lean frames and weight lifting only adds bulk to one's physique. Luckily, more contemporary thinking recognizes the benefits of strength training, for all walks of life, including walkers and those who desire to maintain lean frames.

The previous paragraph alluded to an important, specific qualification. Weight training suggests the use of weight equipment and implements in order to overload one's muscles. Conversely, strength training encompasses a more general view of resistance, meaning that one's body weight can be useful for improving one's strength. Strength training can be performed anywhere, and because it is a natural manipulation of one's body weight, the results are increased strength while maintaining leanness.

Figure 6.1 While strength training is beneficial to walkers, it is not recommended to strength train while walking. Carrying weights or strapping them around one's ankles adds weight to the end of a long resistance arm, putting extra stress on the joints involved and throwing off walking mechanics.

This chapter reviews strength training techniques for training with body weight. Likewise, a second section is dedicated to weight training in a facility. Finally, the chapter concludes with a discussion on exercise prescription (developing a workout routine).

Body Weight Strength Training

Body weight training (BWT) requires minimal equipment, and some workouts can be performed with no equipment at all. Additionally, most BWT exercises require very little space, providing the exerciser with the flexibility to work out just about anywhere. Therefore, BWT is an excellent method of strength training, especially for those who lack the resources to train with weight equipment or who desire to exercise in private.

——— Tip 6.1 ———

The body reacts to stimuli. Even if there are only a few minutes available, employing some body weight training exercises in one's spare time can lead to improved strength. One beneficial practice is to perform a BWT exercise with each commercial while watching television. For example, a two-minute commercial break can provide a bout of thirty seconds of squats, 30 seconds of push-ups, 30 seconds of lunges, and 30 seconds of pull-ups.

BWT improves one's muscular strength, but there is much more gained than strength. Unlike weight training on machines, BWT incorporates more of the balance and body control exhibited in free weight training, often to an even higher degree. In BWT, one must manipulate his or her body in space, which requires body control and balance at multiple angles. Thus, BWT increases motor (muscle) control by increasing attributes such as proprioception (body awareness in space), balance, and neuromuscular control are improved.

© Shutterstock/studio1901

Figure 6.2 Lunges, one of the best body weight exercises for developing total leg strength, are a dynamic, compound exercise that require balance, motor control, and a strong core.

As one can surmise from reviewing Tables 6.1 through 6.3, BWT requires creativity and multiple variations of the same exercise. Because of that, BWT can alleviate the boredom that many people experience when they become accustomed to using the same weight machines workout after workout. For guidelines and suggestions on how to make those variations bring about the greatest improvements, spend extra time reading and postulating on the information presented in the section of this chapter entitled *Developing a Strength Training Routine*.

Table 6.1 Examples of BWT Lower Body Exercises and the Methods to Execute Them.

Exercise	Starting Position	Movement	Comments
Squats	Standing with feet about shoulder width apart, toes straight ahead, and knees balanced over the feet. Hands can be across the chest, on the hips, at the side of the thighs or in front of the body.	Pushing the butt backward while doing so, sit with the butt traversing backward, and with the chest up, still leaning forward some at the hips. Keeping the weight balanced on the heels and midfoot of the feet, the knees should be bent until they are at 90° of flexion. Stand back up to the starting position using the glutes and quadriceps to straighten the knees and hips.	Squats are a fundamental exercise that must be mastered before great proficiency will be achieved in the other lower body exercises. Be sure to keep the eyes focused at about a 35° above their horizon, keeping, and the head up, feet at shoulder width, and the body balanced. To increase intensity, squat with a single leg, rather than with both feet on the ground!
One-Legged Deadlifts	Standing on one leg, the other leg bent so that the knee is at about a 90° angle. Arms are hanging loosely at your sides or the front of your body.	Slowly bend over at the hips with both hands reaching down toward the floor in front of the planted foot. As you are bending, keep your buttocks lifting up and away from the planted foot. The knee of the planted leg may bend slightly, while the other leg moves backward for balance. Stand back up with the buttocks still pushing away and straightening the knee of the planted leg (if bent). It is critical that the buttocks are pushing away and you rotate about your hips. Do not just stand up. Come to a full standing position.	This exercise should be done in a very slow, controlled fashion, being sure to use the buttocks to erect the torso.
Split Squats	Stand in a split leg fashion, one leg forward and one backward, in linear alignment.	Bend both knees, keeping the weight over the center of gravity (balanced in the hips). Bend until the back knee is just about to touch the floor. Push back up with both legs.	Try to strike a balance between pushing back up with both legs. This exercise should be smooth and continuous (no pausing). To increase the intensity, especially in the buttocks, elevate the back leg by putting your foot on a bench (the tip or tops of your toes should be in contact with the bench).

(Continues)

Table 6.1 Examples of BWT Lower Body Exercises and the Methods to Execute Them. (*Continued*)

Exercise	Starting Position	Movement	Comments
Lunges	Stand with both feet at shoulder width, arms to the side, core engaged (tight).	Step forward with one leg, using arms as needed to maintain balance. As soon as the front foot touches the ground, bend both knees and continue to bend until the back knee almost touches the ground. Using the front foot, push forward and down into the floor (at an approximate 45° angle), pushing the body back to the original standing position. From the original position, you can repeat with the same leg or alternate legs.	Lunges can be very intense and will work the buttocks pretty intensely. To add even more intensity, add dips! The dips are performed by pushing up until both legs are nearly straight (like the starting position of split squats), go back down and up, two more times, push back to the lunge starting position after three dips.
Walking Lunges	Same starting position as lunges.	Lunge forward as directed above. Instead of pushing into the floor, push-up and forward, swinging the back leg through until it is in the forward lunge position. Repeat, continuously alternating legs.	In order to add more intensity to this exercise, as you swing the leg forward, lift it high, so that the thigh is parallel to the ground. Bending from this heightened position will increase the eccentric load. You may also add dips to the walking lunges by stepping through on the third dip, using either a low or high leg swing.
Reverse Rotational Lunges	Same starting position as lunges.	Step backward into a lunge position, keeping the hips facing forward, but allowing the foot to cross over the midline of the body. Allow both knees to bend until the back knee almost touches the ground. Return to the starting position, pushing the back foot back and down into the ground. Either repeat with the same leg or alternate legs.	It is critical to keep the hips facing forward, thereby placing the transverse stress on the posterior of the body and generating strain in the lateral (outside) hips and buttocks.
Forward and Back Lunges	Same starting position as lunges.	Lunge forward, as above. When returning, do not stop at the starting position, but lunge backward, either straight back or with the rear rotational lunge protocol. After completing the rear lunge, drive the leg back forward and repeat. For added intensity, use the high knee step through as introduced above.	Forward and back lunges can present a tremendous overload to the body, and that overload can increase with the speed of the movement (the faster the more intense the exercise). When first adding these keep repetitions low in order to focus on maintaining form.

Exercise	Starting Position	Movement	Comments
Step-Ups	Using a stable bench or chair (a padded surface will decrease stability and increase the difficulty/overload), stand with one foot on the bench, the other on the floor.	Using the muscles of the elevated leg only, push up into a standing position (standing on the top leg only). Do not use the lower leg to push off the floor or to stabilize the body when in the up position. Slowly lower the body back down, using the upper leg only. Barely touch the lower foot's toes to the ground (just make contact with a slight touch), and push back up with the upper leg. Do not push off the floor with the lower leg.	This exercise is all about control. Pushing with the lower leg or bouncing will decrease the load and decrease the effectiveness of the exercise.
Physioball Leg Curls	Lying on your back, put both heels up on a physioball (stability ball). Keeping both shoulders in contact with the ground, lift the rest of the body off the ground so that all of the body is suspended between the feet on the ball and the shoulders on the floor.	Push the hips up and continue pushing them up while using the heels to pull the ball back toward the buttocks. Perform the action slowly, making sure that the hips are lifting toward the sky, as this will increase the quality of exercise.	For a real challenge, do these with a single leg, making sure that the body is balanced.
Butt Lifters	Get on all fours (hands and knees), so that the hips are parallel to the ground.	Lift the target leg off of the ground so that the thigh is parallel to the ground. Using only the buttocks, slowly push the heel (try to keep the foot parallel to the floor) toward the sky and providing a strong squeeze of the muscle.	This is another exercise that needs to be performed with control. Be cognizant of the buttocks' contractions, trying to use your mental control of your muscles to maximize the contraction.
Lateral Squat Walks	Stand with your feet slightly wider than should width apart, and squat to a 90° bend in the knees.	While squatting, step to one direction, trailing with the other leg. Continue in that same direction, squatting and stepping out until you reach your desired number of repetitions. When you reach your goal, stop your momentum and go back the other way, leading with the opposite leg.	It is imperative to keep as low a profile as possible. To make this exercise more challenging, a resistance band or tube can be wrapped around the middle of the two feet. This alteration will substantially increase the work of the buttocks.

(Continues)

Table 6.1 Examples of BWT Lower Body Exercises and the Methods to Execute Them. (*Continued*)

Exercise	Starting Position	Movement	Comments
Straight Leg Raises	Sit on the floor, legs out if front of you, back against a wall or supported by your arms (sitting at about a 135° internal hip angle [slightly reclined]. The working leg will be kept straight, while the non-working leg should be bent so that the foot is flat on the floor.	Slowly and with control, lift the straight leg, making sure to keep the quadriceps muscles (front of thigh) contracted. Lift the leg as high as possible, trying to get the thigh parallel to the thigh of the leg still in contact with the ground. Lower the leg back down until just before the heel touches. Repeat.	It is critical to maintain a slow and controlled motion throughout this exercise, while always keeping the quadriceps of the working leg contracted.
Lateral Leg Lifts	Lie on one side, with the legs stacked one on top of the other.	Slowly and with control, lift the top leg as high as possible. Return to the original position, without touching the lower leg. Repeat.	Slow, controlled motions are of critical importance to this exercise delivering the greatest returns.
Calf Raises	Stand on the edge of step, with the balls of the feet on the edge of the step.	Raise up as high as possible on your toes, giving a slight squeeze at the top of the motion, then lower slowly back down, allowing the heels to hang as low as possible. Repeat.	For greater intensity, use only one leg at a time, allowing the other leg to cross behind the working leg or simply hang.
Bent-Knee Calf Raises	Same starting position as calf raises, only with the knees bent about 30°	Keeping the knees bent throughout, raise up as high as possible on your toes, giving a slight squeeze at the top of the motion, then lower slowly back down, allowing the heels to hang as low as possible. Repeat.	For greater intensity, use only one leg at a time, allowing the other leg to cross behind the working leg or simply hang.
Power Skips	Standing position.	Skip with an emphasis of driving up into the air, getting as high off the ground as possible. When making contact with the ground during landing, take off again as soon as possible.	The faster you can leave the ground between skips the better. Put as much force as possible into each takeoff, trying to get as much vertical push as you can.
Pop-Ups	Stand with one foot up on a sturdy bench or box, the other foot on the floor.	Pushing off both feet, explode up into the air, switching the position of the legs in air. Land with the legs opposite the starting position, bending the knee of the elevated knee to 90°. Explode back up to repeat.	The landing and takeoff must happen in as short a period of time as possible, without sacrificing ROM.

Exercise	Starting Position	Movement	Comments
Lateral Bounds	Stand with the feet shoulder width apart.	Push off the ground, using the outside of one foot, moving your body laterally through the air. Land on the opposite leg, absorbing the impact, by bending the knee of the landing leg, with the original leg crossing behind the landing leg. Drive the landing leg back into the ground, and launch back in the opposite direction, repeating.	With maximal effort, it will be possible to cover an area of approximately eight feet. Be sure you have enough room.
Lateral Bench Hops	Stand with one foot on a bench or box, with the other foot off to the side.	Driving off both legs, hop laterally over the bench, alternating feet so that the opposite foot is now up on the bench or box.	Aim for vertical displacement, while quickly moving from side-to-side over the bench or box.
Lateral Bench Jumps	Stand with feet at shoulder width, to one side of a bench or low hurdle.	Hop over the bench or hurdle, bending the knees slightly as you land. Immediately hop back in the other direction.	While you want to get vertical displacement, this exercise is more about agility, being able to change direction quickly.
Box Jumps	Stand in front of a sturdy wooden box or unpadded bench, at least a foot away. Be sure the box/bench is strong.	Jump up and land on the box, bending the knees into a squat as soon as your feet touch the surface. Options: 1) Come back up to standing and step/drop off the box to repeat 2) Jump or drop off the box, land into a squat, come back to standing, turn around and repeat 3) Jump off the box (up and backward), land back into a squat and repeat by exploding out of the squat and jumping back up	The options increase in intensity, as they are listed. Be sure that the movements are smooth and the knees bend to absorb the impact of all landings.
Jump Squats	Same starting position as squats.	Bend the knees, jump straight up by exploding out of the squat trying to reach maximal height. As the feet come back into contact with the ground, bend the knees to absorb the impact, drop to a 90° bend in the knees, explode back up out of the squat to repeat.	The landing and takeoff must happen in as short a period of time as possible, without sacrificing ROM.

(Continues)

Table 6.1 Examples of BWT Lower Body Exercises and the Methods to Execute Them. (*Continued*)

Exercise	Starting Position	Movement	Comments
Jump Lunges	Start in the split squat starting position.	Bend down into the low portion of the spilt squat, push back up; exploding off the floor by pushing off both legs; while reaching peak height, reverse your leg position; land back in split squat position, bending the knees immediately to absorb the impact.	The landing and takeoff must happen in as short a period of time as possible, without sacrificing ROM.
One-Legged Hops with Cycle	Begin by walking fast or jogging	As you step onto the desired leg (the one you want to work), hop into the air, keeping the non-working leg pulled up; pull the working leg up and through a cycle that brings the knee up toward the chest; extend the leg again to impact the ground; absorb the impact by bending the knee; repeat by explosively hopping back up.	This exercise should produce a linear displacement, using your momentum to move you forward.

Table 6.2 Examples of BWT Upper Body Exercises and the Methods to Execute Them.

Exercise	Starting Position	Movement	Comments
Push-Ups	Hands on the floor, just wider than the shoulders, arms extended, legs straight, toes on the floor. Keep the stomach tight, maintaining a straight line from shoulder to the toes.	Bend the elbows to 90°, keeping the body straight and in one line. Push back up until your arms are straight again, elbows not locked.	The most important muscles in this exercise are the abdominal/core muscles, as they maintain the integrity of your body line. The only part of the body that should touch the ground on the low portion of the exercise is the tip of your nose.
Rotational Push-Ups	Same starting position as push-ups.	When coming back up from the down position, lift one hand off the ground and rotate the body to the hand still in contact with the floor. The feet will rotate as well, stacking one on top of the other. The free hand goes up toward the ceiling. Coming back down from the rotated position, the free hand returns to the ground, and the elbow bends immediately. Repeat by alternating the rotation from one side to the other.	Coming down from the rotated position increases the eccentric load on that side of the chest. That load will be eliminated if the elbow does not bend immediately when coming in contact with the floor.

Exercise	Starting Position	Movement	Comments
Military Push-Ups	Same starting position as push-ups.	Perform push-ups, pushing the upper body off the ground, keeping the body straight. While up in the air, clap your hands, and return them to the original position in time to land back on the ground. As soon as the hands touch the ground, the elbows must bend.	Like rotational push-ups, it is imperative that the elbows bend immediately upon the hands making contact with the ground. This will bring about the increased eccentric load desired of this more ballistic exercise.
Triceps Push-Ups	Standard push-up position, with the hands moved under the chest, with the two hands brought together with the thumbs and index fingers placed tip-to-tip, forming a diamond on the inside margin of the fingers.	Perform a push-up, pressing through the hands, but with the elbows bending more than in a standard push-up.	Due to the placement of the hands, the arms will form a diamond when viewed from the front.
Hands-On-Ball Push-Ups	For higher intensity, place the feet on a bench. For lower intensity, keep the feet on the ground. The hands should be placed on the outside edges of the ball, palms in toward the ball.	Perform the push-up, maintaining the grip on the ball by pushing into the ball as the elbows bend.	Using the physioball increases the instability of the exercise, putting greater demand on the abdominal/core muscles as well as the smaller muscles of the upper body used to stabilize the upper body.
Feet-On-Ball Push-Ups	Same starting position as push-ups with the feet placed on a physioball (toes or tops of toes), rather than a bench.	Perform a push-up as you would any other. The core must be more engaged to keep the body in appropriate stability and line.	The instability produced by the ball brings about greater stress on the core of the body.
Two Ball Push-Ups	Put one hand in the middle of one physioball, and the other hand in the middle of the second physioball. The feet should be positioned on a bench or chair.	Perform a standard push-up while maintaining core stability as well as the stability/positioning of the stability balls.	The two ball push-ups place much greater strain on the smaller muscles of the upper body and the core, developing greater total body strength and proprioception.
Three Ball Push-Ups	The same starting position as two ball push-ups only with the feet on a physioball rather than on a bench or chair.	Perform a standard push-up while maintaining core stability as well as the stability/positioning of the stability balls.	The three ball push-up brings about the greatest instability of any BWT exercise presented in these tables, thereby developing tremendous total body strength and proprioception.

(Continues)

Table 6.2 Examples of BWT Upper Body Exercises and the Methods to Execute Them. (*Continued*)

Exercise	Starting Position	Movement	Comments
Chin-Ups/ Pull-Ups	Chin-ups require that the exerciser hang from an overhead bar with the hands at or just wider than shoulder width, hands supinated (turned with the palms away from the body). Pull-ups require that the hands are pronated (palms turned toward the body).	Regardless of hand position, the arms bend to pull the entire body up. Chin-ups require a slight backward tilt in the body, with the elbows being pulled more into the side of the body. Pull-ups result in a slightly higher pull, with the arms closer to the body and traversing further behind the body.	Chin-ups will place greater emphasis on the latissimus dorsi (the wider muscle of the back), where pull-ups will place greater emphasis on the more interior muscles of the back (rhomboids and trapezius) as well as the biceps.
Modified Chin-Ups/ Pull-Ups	Assume the starting position of a chin-up or pull-up, pulling to a bar from a horizontal position, rather than the vertical position of the regular chin-up/push-up. The feet must be placed on the floor, a bench, or a physioball.	Perform the same actions as in a vertical chin-up or pull-up.	The horizontal positioning of the body puts greater stress on the core and greater emphasis on the musculature closer to the spine.
Handstand Push-Ups	Assume a handstand position with your socked feet against a wall.	From the handstand position, lower yourself down to the lowest point possible before your head hits the ground.	Using socked feet will allow you to slide up and down the wall with less friction, making the movement smoother. The greater your strength, the less support you will need from the wall, until you are able to perform the exercise completely freestanding.
Bench/Chair Dips	With the body just in front of a bench or chair, place your hands on the chair or bench, with the fingers over the front part of the chair/bench. The buttocks should be positioned just in front of the bench/chair. The feet should be flat on the floor with knees bent to 90°	Keeping the buttocks back, just in front of the bench or chair, bend the elbows to 90°, then pushing back up to the straight arm position, without locking the elbows.	While performing this exercise, keep the elbows parallel in order to keep the emphasis on the triceps.

Table 6.3 Examples of Core Exercises and the Methods to Execute Them.

Exercise	Starting Position	Movement	Comments
Crunches	Lie on the floor with the feet flat on the floor, knees bent, hands across the chest or at the side of the head. Do not put your hands behind your head. Your chin should be slightly tucked, eyes focused at an approximately 45° angle.	Pull the shoulders up off the ground 3–4 inches, using the abdominal muscles, squeeze for one second, and then ease back down until the shoulder blades touch the ground.	Make your movements slow and controlled to reduce the possibility of strain on your neck.
Double Crunches	From the same crunch position, bring the feet up of the ground with the hips and knees at 90°.	Crunch up while rolling the hips of the ground and up toward the chest.	Pull the hips to the chest and the chest to the knees in synergy, like you are curling up into a ball.
Bicycles	The same starting position as double crunches.	Curl up and twist the upper body to one side bringing the knee on that side up to meet the twisting elbow. Curl back down and repeat to the other side.	Bicycles will work the oblique muscles in the abdominals, giving you the defining lines along the side of your stomach.
Bicycles/ Alternate Leg Extended	The same starting position as bicycles.	Perform a bicycle, but instead of bringing a knee up to meet the crossing arm, extend that leg until it is just above the ground. Curl back down. Repeat to the other side.	Bicycles will work the oblique muscles in the abdominals, giving you the defining lines along the side of your stomach.
Oblique Twists	Assume the double crunch starting position, with your arms across your chest, only resting on the buttocks/tailbone, rather than lying on the back.	Twist the upper torso from side-to-side, with control, going through as much range of motion as possible.	Oblique twists put a greater emphasis on the internal oblique muscles.
Legs Up and Touch	Lie on the back, with the legs straight up in the air. Raise the arms straight up in the air, parallel to the legs.	Crunch up, with control, trying to touch the toes with the finger tips. Lower yourself back down slowly and with control.	This is another crunch, which puts slightly more emphasis on the abdominals, as it produces greater ROM.
Legs Up and Touch to Opposite Toes	Same position as legs up and crunch.	Instead of touching the toes straight on, perform the legs up and touch by reaching the right fingers to touch the left toes, return to the floor, and repeat with the left fingers going to the right toes.	This exercise puts greater emphasis on the oblique muscles, brought on by a greater range of motion.

(Continues)

Table 6.3 Examples of Core Exercises and the Methods to Execute Them. (*Continued*)

Exercise	Starting Position	Movement	Comments
Planks	Assume push-up position, but with the upper body positioned on the elbows, forearms perpendicular to the floor, forearms on the floor, and hands clasped.	Hold the body static for as long as possible. The abdominal and back muscles must contract to support the middle of the body. The body weight needs to be balanced between the legs, core, and shoulders.	There should be absolutely no movement during this exercise. It often helps to imagine that there is a string running from the inside of the belly button through the lower back and up to the ceiling. You want your abdominal muscles to remain constantly drawn up and in.
Side Planks	Lie on your side, and lift the body up, balanced on the bottom foot and the elbow/forearm of the lower arm.	Perform the plank, using the oblique muscles up to pull the lower midsection up into the body. Repeat on the other side.	The same rules apply to this exercise as to the regular plank.
Pelvic Lifts	Assume the starting position of the crunch, with the arms along the side of the body.	Using the abdominal muscles, lift the hips up off the ground with a slow, controlled motion. Bring the hips up to where the body assumes a straight line, from the shoulders to the knees. Very slowly, ease the hips back down until the back almost touches the ground. Repeat.	This exercise works the transverse abdominus, the muscle that is critical to stabilizing the entire core.
Physioball Pendulums	Lie on the back with the arms out to the side, lift the legs straight up, squeezing a physioball between your ankles.	Maintaining control of the physioball, rotate the hips until the leg to which you are rotating almost touches the ground, reverse the motion, raising the hips off the floor as you go back through the starting position, and over to the other side.	This exercise requires extensive control of the forces of motion. Considerable momentum is gained as the legs approach the ground, and overcoming that momentum requires great strength and muscular control.
Elbow Pulls	Assume a plank position with the elbows on a physioball, rather than the floor.	Maintaining the plank, extend your arms, making sure that you keep your forearms pressing down into the ball. Extend as far as possible without straining the upper abdominals too excessively (feel a slight pull and no more). Once the maximum reach is gained, roll the ball back in so that it is under the chest. Repeat	This exercise is a more advanced exercise. It can produce a lot of strain on the abdominals and should only be performed when highly focused.

Exercise	Starting Position	Movement	Comments
Inverted Vs	Assume push-up position with the feet on a physioball.	Using the abdominals, push the hips up into the air (do not use the buttocks), rolling the ball underneath your hips. Your body should look like an upside-down "V."	Use slow, controlled motions, and be sure to focus on only use the abdominal muscles to move the hips.
Knee Pulls	Assume the same position as the Inverted V.	Using the abdominals, roll the hips under the body, bringing the knees to the chest, while rolling the ball underneath the body. Roll the ball back out gently, with control, returning to the starting position.	Use slow, controlled motions, and be sure to focus on only use the abdominal muscles to move the hips.

Strength Training in a Fitness Facility

Because they can be performed anywhere, BWT training exercises are just as effective in a fitness facility as they are anywhere else. In fact, many of the BWT exercises can also be done while holding weights, increasing the balance and workload requirements for the exercise. However, training in a facility allows the exerciser to employ machines and free weights to generate muscular overloads and stresses that one simply cannot do with his or her body weight.

Weight training machines vary in their design, but most machines in fitness facilities have the same utility. Generally speaking, weight machines have adjustable seats and resistance arms (those which are moved when lifting the weight). The resistance arm is attached to a weight stack by a cable that runs across a series of pulleys. A pin is inserted into the weight stack, so that the user may vary the

© Shutterstock/baranq

Figure 6.3 By performing high bar squats, the exerciser is able to increase the stress on the quadriceps and gluteal groups, while also requiring increased core stabilization and an intense static contraction in the shoulders.

Figure 6.4 When using weight training machines, follow the directions printed on the sticker affixed to the machine. Be sure that your axis of rotation (in this exercise, the man's knees) is in line with the axis of rotation of the resistance arm. Also note, in this picture, that the roller, which is the contact point between the moment arm and resistance arm is as far down on the moment arm as it can go (at the front aspect of the ankle [tailor window]), offering the maximum in resistance.

resistance for his or her specific needs. Some companies allow the resistance arms on their machines to move through multiple planes (left to right, front to back, and diagonally) at the same time, providing greater range of motion (ROM) and forcing the user to exhibit greater control. These weight machines offer isotonic exercise, or that type of exercise that allows for a full ROM against a fixed resistance.

There are other, much more specialized, weight machines that allow for isokinetic exercise. Isokinetic exercise requires the use of highly tuned variable resistance that is applied to the resistance arm in order to keep it moving at a constant angular velocity (X degrees per second). In short, the harder one pushes against the lever, the more resistance he or she will encounter, and vice versa. Because the resistance must constantly change in response to the exerciser's effort, the resistance does not come from a weight stack, rather it is controlled by a computer. Thus, isokinetic machines are usually found only in rehabilitation facilities.

Similar to the standard weight training machines, free weights also provide the opportunity to engage in isotonic exercise. The term free weight is very general, and the free weight category of weight training equipment includes Olympic benches and barbells, dumbbells, and kettle bells. Unlike weight machines, which as you recall operate with a series of pulleys and cables, free weights are not attached to any support. Because free weights have no restrictions, the ROM options for working with free weights are virtually limitless. In essence, the only limitation to working with free weights is the exerciser's ability to displace the weight.

Tip 6.2

The exercises in Tables 6.1–6.3 can also be performed in a fitness facility, with dumbbells, kettle bells, or barbells. In order to reduce the risk of injury, be sure that free weight activities that involve heavy weight are performed in the presence of a spotter.

With the freedom that comes from working with free weights, an exerciser has the ability to increase strength, proprioception, and motor control much more efficiently. Because there are no guides or mechanical hinges to control the direction in which a weight will travel, like with machines, the exerciser must balance, support, and control the free weight piece while also moving it through the desired ROM. The extra demands for support place greater neuromuscular stress on the smaller, more intricate muscles with the roles of providing stability and fine motor coordination.

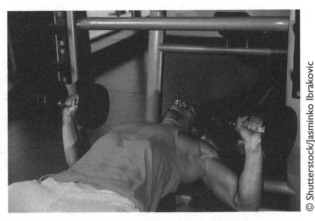

Figure 6.5 While both can dramatically increase strength, the dumbbell bench press (right) provides increased ROM, motor development, and proprioception, even more than the bench press performed with a bar (left).

As exemplified in Figure 6.4, not all free weights are created equally. Those exercises that employ the use of Olympic bars are best suited for trying to increase muscle mass, whereas using dumbbells and kettle bells is better for increasing strength while maintaining a leaner appearance. As well, because they are fairly small and easily stored, dumbbells and kettle bells can be used at home, in order to add extra resistance to the BWT exercises.

Basics of Strength Training

Having a deep knowledge of exercises and what muscles they target is critical to strength training. However, there is more to training than simply having a reservoir of exercises in your memory banks. Developing a strength training routine requires an understanding of training styles, exercise progression, and allowing for adequate recovery and tissue growth.

Generally speaking, exercise prescription follows three basic premises. First, there must be an overload stimulus to bring about an appropriate compensatory growth in strength. Second, the intensity must fluctuate, following an altering easy-hard schedule. Third, the body responds best to workouts that vary to provide different types of overload. Those three premises are governed by the FIT-M principle, which represents the **f**requency, **i**ntensity, **t**ime, and **m**ode of workouts.

Frequency is simply defined as the number of workouts that take place within a week's time. Obviously, the more often one exercises, the greater the overload placed on the body. Some people will take frequency to extremes and will exercise two or more times per day, every day, not allowing the body to recover, often developing overuse injuries. Marathon training is one discipline that walks a very fine line between proper training and overtraining. Many marathoners will run doubles three or four days a week, meaning they will train a total of 10 or 11 workouts per week. While those workouts will prepare them for running 26.2 miles in just over two hours, marathoners are always susceptible to bone and joint injuries or illness. On a more common front, those looking for fitness gains should plan to perform a minimum of four and a maximum of 10 workouts per week.

Intensity is what the name implies, the measure of energy the workout will require. Intensity is one of two variables (time being the other) that must alternate between demanding and less demanding sessions in order to lessen the risks and increase the benefits. Generally speaking, intensity shares an inverse relationship with time, meaning that more intense (physically demanding) a session, the shorter the session will be. Intensity can be defined with various measures, such as weight lifted, heart rate,

---

Tip 6.3

Runners and walkers often use subjective assessment in order to estimate pace. After extensive experience (perhaps years) of walking or running at certain paces, while being provided feedback (e.g. mile splits), well-trained walkers and runners are able to maintain those same paces without any external feedback. Instead, they rely on their subjective evaluations of the efforts they are producing. The best measure of the subjective assessment of intensity is Borg's Rate of Perceived Exertion Scale, a scale that allows the exerciser to quantify his or her effort. A quick Internet search will provide you with a version of the scale that you can use.

---

subjective assessment, and more. When it comes to exercise prescription, intensity is the most manipulated of all of the variables, hence the reason that heart-rate monitors and watches that provide pacing information are so popular.

Time is the length of time (usually in minutes) a workout session lasts. When a workout session is delivered in intervals, each interval session will have a specific time goal, while the time for the overall workout session is also important. As stated in the last paragraph, time is the second variable that must be alternated. A workout session that lasts a long time one day must be followed by a shorter session the next day.

When considering time, one must also consider the cost-benefit ratio. As was stressed in Chapter Four, muscles are more at risk for injury when they are not fully warmed up. Therefore, there is higher risk for injury at the beginning of a workout. As well, a workout needs to provide a minimum of 10 minutes of sustained intensity at heart rates high enough to elicit a training affect. Considering those conditions, exercise sessions that only last 20 to 30 minutes offer fewer rewards (limited training time) and somewhat high risks, leading to a fairly weak cost-benefit ratio. Likewise, workouts that near

© Shutterstock/Maridav

Figure 6.6 Heart rate monitors are useful in measuring intensity, allowing an exerciser to precisely meet the prescribed expectations of a workout.

60 minutes offer the potential for injury due to muscular fatigue. While the benefits of a 60-minute workout are appreciable, the higher risk for injury decreases the cost-benefit ratio. 45-minute workouts present very comparable risks as 30-minute sessions, but they do not present the same risks of fatigue as 60-minute sessions. Meanwhile, the benefits of getting 15 more minutes of exercise over a 30-minute session are considerable. On the other side of the equation, with the body fatiguing as sessions near 60 minutes, performances decline some, thereby lessening the benefits. The decrement of only exercising for 45 minutes, as opposed to 60, therefore, is less than that gained by exercising 45 minutes rather than 30. Thus, the optimal workout session time, from a cost-benefit standpoint, is a 45-minute session.

Mode is sometimes referred to as type (the principle is referred to as FIT-T). Mode is the method of exercising, which, with respect to cardiovascular exercise, can mean running, cycling, walking, swimming, elliptical, skiing, etc. On the strength training side, mode refers more to the style of the workout. Some examples of modes for strength training are circuit training, pyramid workouts, standard workouts (e.g. 3 sets of 5–8 repetitions), time-under-tension workouts, and more. The subsequent paragraphs introduce the various workouts and the unique properties they offer.

Circuit training is a method of training that combines strength training and cardiovascular training in one workout. When performing a circuit training workout, the athlete keeps the weights light, while the repetitions are high. Typically, the athlete will begin the session with a 10- to 15-minute cardiovascular session to increase heart rate. The lifting occurs for a designated time period (usually 30–60 seconds), with no pause or rest. At the end of the lifting interval, the athlete quickly transitions to the next exercise (no more than 15 seconds). After every few lifting sessions, the athlete will interject a session of cardiovascular work to keep the heart rate elevated.

There are many benefits derived from circuit training. First, because the workout should alternate between upper and lower body exercises, with intervals of cardiovascular work mixed in, circuit training delivers a total body, multi-system workout. Second, by mixing weight training and cardiovascular training, the exerciser increases muscular strength and endurance while also providing an environment in which lactic acid is buffered. Finally, circuit training offers a terrific counter to more muscularly intense workouts, providing the opportunity for alternating easy and hard days.

In a similar fashion, high-repetition weight training workouts provide muscular endurance without extensive muscle damage or heavy lactic acid build-up. High-repetition workouts can range from sets that include repetition ranges from 12 to 100 repetitions with very short recovery periods between sets. In order to achieve the higher repetitions, resistance must be kept low (much like walking compared to running). Therefore, while fatigue will set in during the workout, the delayed onset muscle soreness attributed with high-resistance workouts will be considerably less.

Training to increase muscular strength requires heavier weights and greater intensities. Those greater intensities require a greater amount of muscle recruitment, as the more muscle recruited the more work that can be performed. The natural recruitment order of muscle is that type I fibers (slow oxidative) are recruited first, followed by type IIa (slow oxidative glycolytic) fibers, and then type IIb (fast glycolytic) fibers. Type I fibers are those that emphasize muscular endurance and burn both

---

Tip 6.4

Delayed Onset Muscle Soreness (DOMS) is the muscular pain that one feels after a hard workout. The pain is caused by the micro tears that occur in muscle as the result of a high intensity. The micro tears cause inflammation in the muscle tissue, and the greater the number of tears, the greater the pain. DOMS usually sets in around 24 hours post-workout and peaks at approximately 36 hours post-workout. Anti-inflammatory medicines and ice therapy can reduce the pain associated with DOMS.

carbohydrate and fat. Type IIa fibers also burn a combination of fats and carbohydrate, providing both muscular endurance and strength. Finally, type IIb fibers rely on carbohydrate and are the dominant providers of muscular strength and power. It takes considerable overload stress to activate the type IIb fibers, and it is that overload stress that brings about the micro tears mentioned in Tip 6.4.

With strength training protocols requiring heavy weights, it stands to reason that the repetitions performed per set are fewer. The repetitions for strength workouts will generally fall in the range of four to eight repetitions per set. As well, the exerciser will typically perform three to six sets of the exercises with longer rest periods (usually two to three minutes) between sets.

Many people will choose to work in that standard pattern for strength workouts; still others will choose routines that mix a bit of muscular endurance and strength. For example, a popular workout is to employ drop sets, where the exerciser will perform a set with the weight set for what he or she typically will use for eight repetitions, and perform as many repetitions as possible. Once the last repetition is completed, the exerciser racks the weight, decreases the amount of weight, performs another set to fatigue, and repeats the cycle. In performing this workout, the exerciser fatigues the type IIb fibers, followed by the type IIa, and finally the type I.

Another popular routine is to start with higher repetition set and work up in weight with progressive sets, resulting in fewer repetitions with each successive set. For example, the exerciser might start with a 12-repetition set, rest briefly, perform a 10-repetition set, rest a bit longer, perform an eight-repetition set, rest even longer, perform a five-repetition set, rest longer still, and finish with a three-repetition set. In this way, the exerciser pre-fatigues the type I and IIa fibers, forcing even greater reliance on the type IIb fibers in the later sets.

Yet another familiar routine is the pyramid routine. The pyramid routine starts with a set of higher repetitions, usually eight to ten, followed by a set in the five to six-repetition range, then three to four repetitions, and finally one to two. The exerciser then goes back up in repetitions in reverse order. This style of lifting allows a little pre-fatiguing of the type I and IIa fibers, then maximal recruitment of the type IIb, followed by a fatiguing of the type IIa and I in that order.

One does not simply need to alter resistance and repetitions to produce overload. There are also strategies to alter overload through the sequencing of exercise. For example, the greatest gains come from working from the largest muscles down to the smallest. If one fatigues the forearm muscles prior to performing chest or back exercises, the person's grip will be compromised, resulting in the inability to manipulate the heavier weights needed to overload the larger muscles. However, by fatiguing the larger muscle groups first, the smaller muscles will also fatigue, and they will require little to no additional work at the end of the workout session.

Another strategy to alter overload through progression is to employ compound and super sets. Compound sets are two (or more [giant sets]) exercises, involving the same muscle groups, done back-to-back without rest. The first exercise is done to pre-fatigue the larger muscles so that they will

---

Tip 6.5

Many people suggest that the back is a hard group of muscles to work. If you want to increase the size and strength of your back muscles, try a compound set that really acts more like a drop set. Perform a set of chin-ups to fatigue and then shift to pull-ups. The pronated (palms forward) grip of the chin-ups emphasizes the latissimus dorsi and trapezius muscles (larger back muscles) while limiting the role of the posterior shoulders and biceps. Supinating (palms toward you) the grip allows the rhomboids, subscapular, and bicep muscles to more fully engage, allowing for additional reps and greater work for the back.

fatigue in greater balance with the smaller muscles in the second exercise. For example, a compound set for the chest group would be chest flies and the bench press. Performing chest flies first will fatigue the pectoral muscles (major and minor) to a degree that they will be slightly compromised while performing the bench press. The bench press also incorporates the anterior shoulders and triceps, which typically fatigue faster than the pectoral muscles. By pre-fatiguing the pectorals, they will fatigue at a rate similar to the shoulder and triceps muscles, resulting in greater overload for all of the muscles involved.

In contrast to compound sets, super sets employ the pairing of antagonistic muscles working back-to-back without rest. As was discussed in Chapter Four, muscles are generally paired as agonists and antagonists, such as the chest and back or quadriceps and hamstrings. In a super set, one muscle is worked while its antagonist relaxes. Once that exercise is done, the exerciser moves immediately into an exercise for the antagonist muscle, forcing the original agonist to relax (reciprocal inhibition). In employing supersets, an exerciser is able to work two muscle groups while decreasing the rest time required and bringing about a deeper relaxation of the muscles during recovery. More work can be done in a shorter period of time, increasing the overall intensity of the workout, thereby providing the requisite overload.

Another aspect of increasing muscular performance is the ability to generate power. Power is defined as work/time, meaning that if one does the same amount of work in less time, more power is generated. There are many ways to train to increase power, but the two most popular are power lifting and plyometric exercises. Power lifts include the power clean, hang clean, and snatch. They are typically performed in sets of one to three repetitions, with very explosive phases throughout the exercise and long recovery sessions between sets.

Plyometric exercises are jumping exercises in which there is a flight phase, followed by a very short amortization (ground contact) phase that transitions into a takeoff phase. The emphasis for plyometric exercises is placed on decreasing the amortization phase, which is the time from which the foot (feet) first comes in contact with the ground to the time at which the foot leaves the ground again. It is critical

Figure 6.7 The snatch is a highly explosive and precise exercise that requires a great deal of power. As one can see, the entire body works in concert to generate the power needed to perform the snatch properly. (This could also be the second pull of the power clean, with the difference being in how the weight is caught.)

that the exerciser goes through the appropriate ROM in the amortization phase and does not sacrifice ROM for speed. The most popular plyometric exercise is running.

The most unique characteristic about power exercises is that they emphasize a fast and highly forceful eccentric load on the body. The more intense the eccentric component of an exercise is, the greater will be the overload, thus the greater will be the muscle damage. Therefore, if done right, one will not need high volumes of repetitions to fully tax the body. Power lifting sessions should be closely regulated to ensure that mechanics are not sacrificed, and plyometric sessions should never exceed 150 footfalls (per foot), regardless of the experience of the exerciser.

━━━━━━ Tip 6.6 ━━━━━━

Power exercises are all about speed, but it is also important to perform the exercise through the full range of motion and with proper form. To not do so can lead to limited gains or injury, respectively. It is important to consider the weight to speed balance that brings about the most power. The weights used should be heavy enough to generate good resistance, but light enough that they can be moved quickly through space, with control.

Developing a Strength Training Routine

Planning a strength training routine is not a simple task. Often, many people fail to achieve the gains for which they are hoping, because they fail to consistently provide novel overload for their muscles. Simply, they get stuck in the same routine, day-by-day, week-by-week. Without stimulation, muscles become stagnant and growth is limited. Therefore, to get the most out of training, it is imperative to present the body with a variety of stimuli. Once again the FIT-M principle must be at the forefront.

One of the best ways to ensure that change happens regularly is to follow a planning model that has the change integrated with its foundation. The best representation of such a model, in the area of exercise prescription, is the periodization model. Periodization is organized in cycles, and those cycles are categorized as microcycles, mesocycles, or macrocycles. Microcycles are the shortest of the cycles, and multiple microcycles come together to form mesocycles. Likewise, multiple mesocycles form macrocycles. A macrocycle, being that it is comprehensive and cumulative, usually transcends long time frames. Often, it is best to plan for macrocycles that last a year.

In the classic, linear periodization scheme, the microcycles are highly organized. The first microcycle is hypertrophy, which is a term that typically means increase in muscle size. However, in this case, hypertrophy indicates a period of high volume. The second microcycle is strength, in which the exerciser follows a more traditional strength enhancing workout. The third microcycle is power, which features high-intensity exercises completed in very short periods of time to maximize power output. The final microcycle is the taper/maintenance cycle, in which the exerciser decreases frequency and time, while maintaining enough intensity to keep the neurological gains from reversing while allowing the muscles to fully recover.

As previously stated, the hypertrophy microcycle is used to generate very high volumes of exercise. That volume produces so much overload that the muscles break down and do not fully recover, leading to a degradation of performance. In the hypertrophy cycle, the frequency and time of workouts both

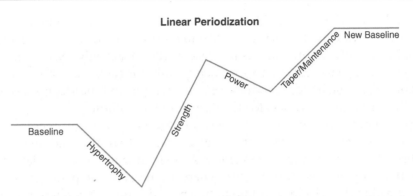

Figure 6.8 Linear Periodization involves the use of structured microcycles. The microcycles bring about muscle breakdown that decreases performance, followed by overcompensation, resulting in muscle synthesis, which increases performance.

generally increase, meaning the exerciser works out more often and for longer periods of time spent on each muscle group during each session.

The exerciser transitions out of the hypertrophy microcycle and into the strength microcycle. In the strength microcycle, the exerciser will reduce the frequency of the workouts as well as the time spent within each muscle group. Instead, intensity is ramped up and the exerciser follows a more traditional strength training regimen as described above. The harder, more compact sets produce additional micro tears in the muscles, but the longer time periods between exercise sessions, and the lower number of repetitions performed, allow the body to recover and even get stronger. During this microcycle, the body overcompensates in repairing itself, trying to protect itself from being overwhelmed in the same fashion again. By the end of the strength microcycle, the exerciser should experience an increase in performance over that which he or she had prior to beginning the hypertrophy microcycle.

The power microcycle is used to break down the body's musculature again. In this microcycle, the emphasis is on intensity, which is increased when the resistance is set at a moderately hard level, but the speed of movement is dramatically increased. As previously stated, there is a great emphasis placed on high-speed eccentric actions, which produce many deep micro tears in the muscle fibers. Three intense power workouts per week should be sufficient to produce the performance decrement needed to illicit the desired overcompensation during the next microcycle.

The final microcycle is the maintenance or taper microcycle. The difference between maintenance and taper is in the destination that awaits the end of the microcycle. If there is a competition at hand, the exerciser is focusing on tapering, meaning that the recovery must be absolutely maximized. A maintenance session, which leads directly into another mesocycle of periodization training, can allow for slightly more aggressive exercise sessions on the workout days. The important concept to keep in mind during this microcycle is that the muscles will not lose what was gained by providing some extra rest. While most take only 48 hours between exercise sessions targeting a muscle group, during this microcycle, it is completely appropriate to take 72 hours of rest between workouts; even 96 hours of recovery is acceptable. Additionally, the workout sessions should not be long. There should be enough exercise done to produce a stimulus (one to two sets per exercise), without producing so much stress that the muscles will experience high levels of damage. The critical takeaway from this microcycle is that the body must be fully recovered and rested.

Like microcycles, mesocycles should progressively improve as they culminate into a macrocycle. Therefore, the mesocycles should be designed around one or two target events per year. For example, a marathoner might run only two marathons per year. If they are evenly spaced, the marathoner would designate two pairs of two mesocycles to specifically train for each marathon. The first mesocycle in each pairing should focus on building endurance and strength, and the second should be more focused on fine-tuning the marathoner's fitness for the designated marathon.

Many people do not like following extremely structured workout protocols, and still others tend to get bored repeating similar routines workout after workout. To that end, undulating periodization requires less absolute structure and more variety. As the name implies, undulating periodization is a training model that emphasizes constant flux. There are no absolute patterns or structured progressions. In working within the principles of undulating periodization, the exerciser rotates through hypertrophy, strength, and power workouts at will, constantly changing the order and style of the workouts to provide unique experiences to which the muscles must respond.

Aside from the variety it offers, the true beauty of undulating periodization is that it allows enough flexibility to factor in important performance events without sacrificing the long-term plan. For example, a college basketball team will play two to three games a week during its season. One might consider that there is no time to engage in strength training workouts, but with undulating periodization, it may be possible to squeeze in a couple of performance-enhancing workouts each week.

Let's look at a two-week example. In week one, the basketball team has games on Wednesday and Saturday. The Wednesday game is against a notoriously underwhelming team, while the Saturday game is against last year's conference champion, and every conference game is treated as a must win. In the second week, the team has regional games on Monday and Thursday, and another conference game on Sunday. In the first week, knowing that DOMS does not peak until 36 hours post workout, the team can have a pretty intense strength workout on Tuesday and still be able to handle the weaker Wednesday opponent. However, the team needs to be well-rested heading into Saturday's contest. Therefore, the team might participate in a very light maintenance workout on Friday. Because the Saturday game will be intense, the team can count that as a power workout, meaning there will not be another workout before the next game on Monday. However, a hypertrophy workout on Tuesday will provide some motor stimulation without too much muscle damage, allowing for a full recovery by Thursday's game. With the second week's games all having some import, all three will probably elicit some strength and power responses for the body; therefore, the one hypertrophy workout should be enough to maintain the training effect.

Like the basketball example, an individual will have weeks when life gets overwhelming. The week's stresses can produce hormone and heart rate responses similar to those evoked by strength and power workouts. The best course of action is to dial down the intensity of the week's sessions and focus on only one or two hypertrophy workouts that week. When things become less demanding the next week, the person's motivation, attention to detail, and energy can be maximized in strength and power workouts.

Both linear and undulating periodization produce great results and one is not better than the other. While undulating periodization is good for those who need variety, linear periodization is better for those who seek consistency and more direct feedback on their progress. In providing the latter, linear periodization is a better model for the highly goal-oriented, as short-term goals are easily defined and quantified in the linear periodization model.

In Perspective

Rachel wants to gain strength without developing muscular bulk. She does not want to get bored or too routine, so she has developed a plan to change up her workouts regularly. She has decided to use undulating periodization. Her plan is to follow the same rotation every two weeks, strength training four days per week. Here is her plan.

Week One:

Day 1: Hypertrophy workout (total body circuit training with body weight exercises, working 45 seconds, 15 seconds to change exercises. 60 minutes total workout time).

Day 2: Power workout (plyometric workout 120 total foot touches of varying plyometric exercises).

Day 3: Rest day

Day 4: Strength workout (total body workout with 5 leg exercises and 6 upper body exercises, 3 sets of 8 per exercise, with 1:00 recovery between sets)

Day 5: Rest day

Day 6: Hypertrophy workout (100 continuous reps per each exercise, 4 upper body, 4 leg)

Day 7: Rest day

Week Two:

Day 1: Strength workout (drop sets 6 leg exercises and 3 upper body exercises)

Day 2: Rest day

Day 3: Power workout (plyometric workout with weighted vest [10#], 10 sets of 12 jump squats with 3:00 rest between sets)

Day 4: Hypertrophy workout (total body circuit training with weight machines at the gym. 20 repetitions per exercise, 3 circuits through all machines)

Day 5: Rest day

Day 6: Power workout (12 sets of 10 one-legged hops with cycle, with 3:00 recovery between sets)

Day 7: Rest day

Conclusion

There will always be critics who question whether endurance athletes (e.g. runners and walkers) should train to increase strength or muscle mass. However, no matter the vocation, recreation practices, or interests, every person can benefit from increased strength. The key to gaining strength is in providing the body with an aggressive overload followed by sufficient recovery time.

Strength training does not require a huge monetary investment. The body can provide all of the resistance and leverage one needs to increase strength. What is required is a consistency and dedication, qualities that will be discussed in even greater detail in Chapter Nine.

In Practice

Strength training can greatly improve one's walking performance. Strength gains are more permanent after eight weeks of training. Beginning with disseminating what goals you would hope to achieve within the eight-week period, and based on what you have read in this chapter, develop a workout that you think you might follow over the next eight weeks. You do not need to write specific exercises (with the exception of suggesting specific plyometric workouts as in the example). Make sure your workout references the FIT-M principle.

Follow this template:

Goal 1: _____

Goal 2: _____

Workout

ADVANCED WALKING TRAINING

Introduction

Some who read this book may be content to get out and walk for 30–45 minutes in order to promote a positive lifestyle through regular exercise and self-efficacy (the confidence in one's ability to maintain a behavior). If that is your goal, this chapter may not be the most applicable. However, if at any time in your life you want to increase your fitness, this chapter will become invaluable. As you learned in Chapter V, there are many biomechanical aspects to a person's walking gait. As complex as proper biomechanics training might be, training for physiological performance is even more complex.

As was learned in Chapter Three, there are many ways in which to assess one's physical fitness, particularly cardiovascular fitness. However, assessment does very little good if the feedback is not used as a rationale for maintaining or improving one's fitness profile. That profile is a cumulative summary of three components, which are aerobic endurance, anaerobic threshold, and aerobic power (VO_{2max}).

Aerobic endurance can be simply defined as the body's ability to maintain a submaximal level of aerobic exercise over an extended period of time. Because the goal is to remain consistent for a long period of time, the intensity will remain fairly low throughout the exercise session. Aerobic endurance sessions will typically last from about one-half of an hour to several hours, with intensity generally staying in the range of 50–60% of maximum heart rate.

Anaerobic threshold is the point at which lactic acid increases, exponentially, within the bloodstream. As can be recalled from Chapter Four, lactic acid, which leads to fatigue, increases when the workload exceeds the ability to distribute oxygen to working muscles, making the muscles work anaerobically. Being directly related to oxygen delivery, the former sentence refers to complications of VO_{2max}. However, anaerobic threshold depends on more than simply oxygen delivery, as the process of lactate buffering also plays into the regulation of blood lactate accumulation. Therefore, those who buffer lactate more efficiently will fatigue less, increasing performance. While buffering requires oxygen, it also relies on lactate being shuttled to the more aerobic muscle fibers (typically the type I and, to a lesser extent, type IIa), at which point oxygen is introduced to produce water and pyruvate. That shuttling is dependent upon the efficiency of the cardiovascular system, which is strengthened through moderately intense and shorter, repetitive bouts of exercise. Each exercise bout should be followed by a short recovery period, so as to keep the heart rate at a moderately high level.

VO_{2max} is the body's ability to take in and distribute oxygen to the muscles, and it sets the genetic limit for the ability to perform in cardiovascular events. Through training, one can increase VO_{2max} to that genetic limit, thereby allowing one to perform to his or her genetic potential. Training to increase VO_{2max} requires high-intensity training in short bouts with slightly longer recovery periods than what are required for anaerobic threshold training. The higher intensity places greater demand on the bigger, more anaerobic muscle fibers (types IIa and IIb), which leads to greater production of lactic acid. The increase in lactic acid must be offset, so the recovery periods need to be active, thereby allowing greater shuttling of the lactic acid to the type I fibers for buffering. In essence, each short recovery period is a miniature EPOC session, which allows for a more natural recovery of the cardiovascular system and allows for the repetition of the high-intensity work.

While VO_{2max} determines the genetic limit to maximum physical performance, it is not necessarily the greatest predictor of performance. Instead, anaerobic threshold is more likely to influence performance in cardiovascular activity. For example, let's look at two people with the same VO_{2max}, say 62 ml $O_2 \cdot kg^{-1} \cdot min^{-1}$, which is a very good capacity. If person one's anaerobic threshold is 67% of his or her VO_{2max}, and person two's anaerobic threshold is 79% of his or her VO_{2max}, person two will be able to work at a much higher level of intensity than person one (12%, 7.44 ml $O_2 \cdot kg^{-1} \cdot min^{-1}$, or 1.5 mph faster), before exponentially increasing lactic acid in the blood. Using those numbers, if the two people were running miles at anaerobic threshold, which is typical of a race effort, it would take person one about 25.5 minutes to complete the run, while person two would finish in just over 21 minutes. If the event was a longer one, aerobic endurance would also factor into the discussion, as the two people would have to be able to resist fatigue for a longer period of time. Because of this complex relationship, maximum performance can only be achieved by blending all three components of cardiovascular performance. The following sections provide greater detail about how to train within each component, understanding that no one component works completely alone.

Training for Endurance: Long Slow Distance (LSD) Training

LSD training is exactly what the name implies, exercising for long time periods at low intensities. LSD training is best for developing aerobic endurance as well as muscular endurance in the legs. It is important to note that the small muscles of the foot and lower leg are put under a great deal of stress over long distances. Hence, while with every training session those muscles are getting stronger, building up resistance to strains and other soft tissue injuries, LSD workouts must build up slowly (no more than a 10% increase per week).

To benefit from LSD, one must commit to a minimum of 30 minutes of exercise at a heart rate that is high enough to elicit a training effect. Typically, the desired heart rate range for LSD training is 60–75% of maximum heart rate (HR_{max}). HR_{max} is found by taking one's age and subtracting it from 220; thus a 20-year-old person would have a theoretical HR_{max} of 200 beats per minute (bpm). To find the optimal LSD training range, one would multiple 0.60×200 to get the low-limit heart rate of 120 bpm. Then, 0.75×200 would set the high-limit heart rate at 150 bpm. What should be obvious is that shorter walks (those close to 30 minutes) should generate heart rates closer to the higher limit, while longer walks can be performed closer to the lower limit. More conditioned walkers can easily maintain the upper limit heart rates for walks that last for hours.

When considering an LSD workout, it is important to consider the risk-reward ratio associated with exercise. Of course, there is always reward in exercise, and risk is ever present as well. Even with a proper warm-up, there is always an increased risk in the beginning phases of a workout, as muscles and joints are at higher risk for injury until homeostasis is achieved and the body is fully adapted to the metabolic, cardiovascular, and neuromuscular demands placed upon it by the environment (temperature, walking surface, walking tempo, proprioception, etc.). Therefore, risk is higher in the first 10 to 15 minutes of exercise. Likewise, it takes a while for the body to start realizing the full benefits of an exercise session, with those benefits typically occurring from the 15-minute mark on. As well, with longer bouts of exercise, muscular and even joint fatigue will set in, which increases the risk of injury. In bouts of exercise that near 60 minutes or more, the risk for fatigue-related injury sets in.

Given what we know about risk and reward in LSD workouts, the optimal workout time length should be logical. 30-minute sessions offer a fair share of reward, but the time period for increased

Figure 7.1 Long, slow distance walking can be more entertaining if shared with others. Inviting others on a long walk can decrease boredom and lead to longer, more simulating walks.

risk is fairly equal to the time period for the reward. At 60 minutes, the rewards are high, but due to fatigue, risk starts to increase as well. 45-minute workout sessions offer twice as much reward time as 30-minute sessions without incurring too much additional risk for injury. Similarly, 45-minute sessions do not present the same level of risk as sessions that approach 60 minutes in length. Therefore, logic tells us that sessions of roughly 45 minutes of exercise give us the most reward for the risk. By the same token, for longer workouts, 90-minute sessions are better than those lasting 60 minutes or two hours.

In general, LSD days should encompass about 20% of one's total weekly mileage. Therefore, LSD days should not be confused with easy days. They are meant to provide a volume overload to the musculoskeletal and cardiovascular systems, and one must allow for recovery from LSD workouts just as one would for workouts of higher intensity. Please refer to the end of this chapter for more detailed information on how to vary one's training to maximize performance, regardless of your goals.

Training to Improve Anaerobic Threshold: Threshold Training

The first time I heard the term "tempo" was in my first cross-country interval workout at SUNY College at Cortland. My coach, Dr. Jack Daniels, one of the world's foremost experts on distance running was putting us through our first "speed session" and it was a tempo workout. During that session, I did not fully understand what he meant by tempo, and since we were doing speed work, I figured it just meant up tempo. After all, in high school, I simply knew that speed days were fast, and easy days were slow. That's the difference between one coach being a librarian and the other being an internationally acclaimed scientist. My ignorance did not last long.

To sit through a Monday team meeting with Jack was to sit through a crash course in the precise manipulation of exercise physiology to maximize running performance, and after the first such meeting, I realized that there were different levels of training that targeted different aspects of cardiovascular performance. It was in my first team meeting that I started to understand that tempo training had a precise goal and exact specifications, and that tempo training was more commonly known as threshold training. (I also learned, then, that LSD was not simply an easy day.) The question begs to be asked, however. With all of this talk about running, why does anaerobic threshold matter to a person who is walking for fitness?

As you will recall from the beginning of this chapter, anaerobic threshold is critical to performance differences between two individuals with statistically similar VO_{2max} ratings. In other words, the higher the person's anaerobic threshold is, the higher will be the performance. This should make sense, as the higher your capacity for performing is, without generating excessive lactic acid accumulation in the blood, the greater will be the work you can perform without experiencing undo fatigue. Thus, if you are trying to improve your fitness, the ultimate goal is to be able to improve your ability to walk at faster speeds with less fatigue.

Precisely determining anaerobic threshold usually requires a graded exercise test, blood samples, and some statistical analysis. However, you can estimate that your anaerobic threshold is going to fall somewhere in the range of 75–85% of HR_{max}. Using the same example as earlier in the chapter, we know that a 20-year-old person's HR_{max} is 200 bpm, and 75% of that is 150 bpm. The upper limit for that same person's threshold training is 0.85×200 or 170 bpm.

That heart rate range suggests one logical appraisal of threshold workouts; to reach the upper limit, one will have to be walking at a very high rate of speed, or a treadmill may be necessary to increase the elevation. As you learned in Chapter Five, the best way to produce higher heart rates on a treadmill is to walk at a moderately high speed while also setting the grade at a moderate level. A treadmill is also beneficial in that it allows for greater control over speed, environmental conditions, and safety.

Threshold workouts can vary in style between a longer sustained workout and one that is intermittent. The intermittent threshold workouts require moderately long intervals with short recovery periods between each interval. The threshold segments should typically last between four and six minutes, but they can last up to 10 to 12 minutes. For the former, the recovery period should be one minute, while for the latter, the recovery should be three to four minutes. Again, recovery periods need to be active in nature in order to maximize lactic acid buffering. The number of intervals performed depends upon the desired length of the workout. Typically, a threshold workout should amass three to four miles of work at the threshold level, so the number of intervals would be determined by the goal mileage divided by the distance covered in each interval (e.g. nine intervals of 4 to 6 minutes or two to three intervals of 10 to 12 minutes). Because there is a recovery period between intervals, the goal would be to reach a heart rate closer to the 85% limit during the threshold segments.

In contrast to the intermittent threshold workouts, sustained threshold training sessions are done in one long interval with no rest or recovery. As such, sustained threshold sessions are best done at heart rates in the lower half of the target range (i.e. 75–80% of HR_{max}). When performing sustained threshold workouts, it is critical to monitor heart rate, as you want to ensure that you are working hard enough without exceeding the threshold. Failing to maintain an appropriate heart rate can lead to decreased performance benefit (a heart rate that was too low) or injury (a heart rate that was too high). Using a heart rate monitor can help you maintain the precise heart rate required for threshold training.

In addition to the importance of maintaining a precise heart rate, warm-up and cool down are critical to the success of a threshold workout. As discussed in Chapter Four, warm-up allows you to increase your muscle flexibility, temperature, respiration, and heart rate gradually, thereby decreasing the risk for injury and limiting the oxygen deficit experienced at the beginning of the workout. As well, cool down allows for the removal of metabolic waste products and shortens recovery time.

Training to Improve VO₂ₘₐₓ: Interval Training

Interval training is used to increase VO_{2max}, which means that the athlete is improving the ability to take in and deliver oxygen to the working muscles. There are several factors that lead to increased oxygen delivery. Those factors include cardiac output, stroke volume, capillary density, and red blood cell count. Prior to discussing the actual method of interval training, each of those factors must be explained.

Cardiac output (Q) is quickly defined as the amount of blood circulated by the heart in one minute. Q is the product of heart rate (HR) and stroke volume (SV), and it varies, depending upon the intensity of the exercise and fitness of the athlete. A specific exercise intensity results in a specific VO_2 requirement, meaning that walking at 4 mph requires the same relative amount of oxygen, regardless of a person's fitness. Therefore, Q is the same. Cardiovascular training (training), however, influences aspects of a person's physiology to bring about changes in SV.

SV is the amount of blood pumped out of the heart's left ventricle with each beat, and training has a direct, profound impact on SV. Simply stated, one of the most important results of training is the increase seen in SV. There are two variables that influence SV, and they are chamber volume of the left ventricle and ejection fraction.

The size of the left ventricle influences chamber volume. With training, the left ventricle's chamber increases in size (left ventricle hypertrophy [LVH]), thereby allowing the left ventricle to fill with more blood prior to each beat. The more blood there is within the ventricle, the more blood that can go out to the body and supply the working muscles with O_2 and nutrients, per beat. Despite the volume of blood that is sent to the body, with each beat, there is always a residual amount left behind. The amount of blood that is sent out of the heart, or stroke volume, divided by the total amount of blood prior to the ventricle's contraction, is known as the ejection fraction.

The heart is a muscle; thus, it is strengthened in the same fashion as any other muscle, being subjected to overload. Overloading the heart causes an increase in the contractility of the muscle fibers (strength), thus creating more forceful contractions. The more forceful contractions increase the ejection fraction, thereby increasing stroke volume. When you combine the results of increased volume due to LVH and increased ejection fraction, there is a profound impact on SV.

Tip 7.1

The heart's muscle fibers can be stimulated to become thicker, which typically happens through training with a high level of strain, brought on by high-resistance loads (heavy weight training). The thickening of the heart's musculature is also called LVH, but it is much less desirable than volume hypertrophy.

Because Q relies on both HR and SV, an increase in one of those two variables can lead to a decreased reliance on the other variable. Therefore, an increase in SV will lead to a decreased HR to bring about the same Q. Consequently, a trained athlete will be able to produce the same Q as an untrained person, at a reduced HR, making the heart a more efficient muscle. Greater efficiency results in fewer metabolic wastes being produced and decreased fatigue. Given these outcomes, it stands to reason that one of the primary objectives of training is to increase SV.

In addition to SV, training increases the number of capillaries in the lungs and muscles (increased capillary density) and the number of red blood cells circulating through the body. Increased capillary density leads to more opportunities for gas exchange, meaning that more oxygen can be brought in to and more carbon dioxide can be sent out of the muscles. By increasing the amount of oxygen in the muscles, a person can remain more metabolically aerobic, decreasing the accumulation of lactic acid and reducing fatigue.

Not only does training increase the delivery of oxygen, it increases the size and contractility of the muscle fibers in the trained muscles. The greater the muscle fiber size is, the greater will be the oxygen uptake, resulting in more oxygen being used. It is that increased utilization that increases VO_{2max}.

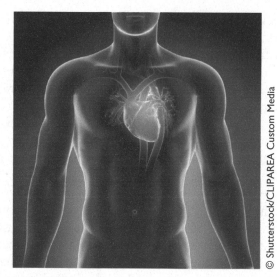

Figure 7.2 Increasing the size and strength of the heart's left ventricle leads to a greater stroke volume, making the heart more efficient and resulting in fewer heart beats per minute and greater cardiac efficiency.

Figure 7.3 Race walking evokes heart rates that are high enough to bring about increases in VO_{2max}. However, race walking is a difficult sport to master, and it produces a tremendous amount of stress on the hip joints.

Ultimately, the goal of interval training sessions is to overload the musculoskeletal and cardiovascular systems to a degree that produces the aforementioned changes. Therefore, the intensities must be very high. Typically, interval training sessions will generate heart rates in the 85–95% of HR_{max} range. Using that same 20-year-old person, the heart rate ranges for interval training will be from 170 to 190 bpm. Those heart rates suggest a very important complication. With the exception of elite race walkers, it may be physically impossible for a person to generate and sustain walking speeds that will bring about heart rates that fall within the suggested range.

Figure 7.4 Despite different mechanics, running is a terrific way to increase VO_{2max}, anaerobic threshold, and muscular strength. A track is the perfect location to run intervals, as tracks absorb impact, allow for precisely measured distances, and flat surfaces.

Despite the challenge that the aforementioned heart rate range presents, there is a very viable solution for increasing VO_{2max}. Regardless of the biomechanical differences between running and walking that were explored in Chapter Five, the best way to improve VO_{2max} is to introduce some running into one's daily workouts. That claim is based on one simple premise. Running is a more ballistic and dynamic form of exercise than walking, and with that, more muscle is incorporated, meaning there is a greater demand for oxygen, resulting in higher heart rates.

Due to their higher intensity, the duration of interval sessions should be less than the duration of the intermittent segments in threshold training. As well, the purpose of interval workouts is to build strength and maximize performance, suggesting that the body needs to be more recovered between intervals. Therefore, interval sessions should be no more than five minutes in length, and there should be a 1:1 ratio of work to recovery. Those restrictions aside, there are many ways in which one can conduct an interval training session.

Interval sessions are easily accomplished on a track, and a rubberized, all-weather surface provides extra cushioning during the running sessions. A novice runner will benefit greatly from the extra cushioning, as the cushioning can lessen musculoskeletal stress, thereby lessening the risk for and severity of muscle, bone, and joint injuries. The flat, uniform service is also valuable for decreasing the risk for tripping, rolling an ankle, or exposing the legs to joint stress caused by angular displacement. Additionally, measuring distances traveled with each aspect of an interval workout is easily accomplished on a track. However, tracks don't always offer pleasant sceneries to decrease boredom, and access to a track is not a reality for some.

A potentially more interesting and convenient way to conduct an interval workout is to hit the road for a fartlek workout. Fartlek workouts incorporate easy–hard training principles in one continuous exercise session. A fartlek workout should begin with a walking warm-up of 10–15 minutes. Once the body is sufficiently warmed up, a running session should ensue. During this running session, it is critical that the heart rate gets into the desired range between the two- and three-minute mark. The interval should last four to five minutes, followed by an equal length (four to five minutes) of walking to allow the heart rate to recover while also allowing the body to buffer some lactic acid. It is best for the heart rate to get close to 120 bpm by the end of the recovery period. This sequence should repeat for up to five intervals, and the workout should end with an extended walking cool down.

While the mechanics of walking and running are not identical, they are highly complementary. However, there is a caveat that must be considered. Running increases the stress on both the muscles and bones. Therefore, the transition to running must be slow and deliberate. Once acclimated to the stresses, there is much to be gained in terms of muscular development and bone density. The increased strength gained from running will lead to an increased walking stride length, resulting in faster walking paces. Further, the increased bone loading will improve bone density and decrease the risk of stress injuries in bones.

———— Tip 7.2 ————

Running intervals can lead to increased muscular strength and bone density, but the transition to running must be slow and deliberate. Start with only a couple of running intervals in the first session, and add no more than one additional interval each week.

Sample Walking Workout Schedule

Developing an appropriate walking workout requires an open mind and plenty of critical thought. The easy–hard principle must always be considered, and hard workouts must provide the appropriate overload to bring about the desired changes in performance. Table 7.1 provides an example of a four-week cycle of training that could be used to start to improve performance. As should be observed in the table, there is an increase in the intensity of the workouts with each progressive week. As well, the first half of the program is characterized by relatively light workouts (in terms of frequency and time), while in the fourth week, a third workout during the week signifies an increased effort to bring about performance gains. An appropriate performance training program should demonstrate consistency while also stressing variability in the intensity and duration of the workout sessions. As one becomes more proficient in performance training, the variability and creativity expressed in the workouts can be increased. [Insert Table 7.1]

Referring back to Table 7.1, the schedule provided is fairly aggressive and would align with a goal of improving one's fitness in very short order. Someone looking to improve his or her fitness a little more conservatively would be best served with one day of LSD and one day of more intense training. If a less aggressive plan is in order, it is highly advised to space out the LSD and performance workout sessions with two and three days' rest between them, on either side. As well, workout prescription/design should be tailored to each individual, so it is important to use Table 7.1 as a guide to designing a workout prescription, keeping in mind one's goals as well as current fitness levels.

When considering how to adjust workouts, it is important to keep the FIT-M principle, which was introduced in Chapter Six, in mind. While the mode is not likely to change much, it has been suggested that running can be used to stress the body for the greatest performance gains. The most likely source of overload will come from intensity, with time and frequency being used to augment the effect of intensity. Remember to keep in mind the importance being patient and deliberate when making changes to any aspect of the FIT-M principle.

Table 7.1 An Example of a Four-Week Cycle of Training for a Peron Starting to Train for Performance.

Sunday	Monday	Tuesday	Wednesday	Thursday	Friday	Saturday
LSD (20% of target mileage goal)	Easy day or day off (a short walk or warming up and stretching)	Threshold (3–4 intervals at 75–85% of HR$_{max}$)	Easy day or day off (a short walk or warming up and stretching) walk or warming up and stretching)	Easy day or day off (a short walk or warming up and stretching)	Threshold (3–4 intervals at 75–85% of HR$_{max}$)	Easy day or day off (a short walk or warming up and stretching)
LSD (20% of target mileage goal)	Easy day or day off (a short walk or warming up and stretching)	Threshold (4–5 intervals at 75–85% of HR$_{max}$)	Easy day or day off (a short walk or warming up and stretching)	Easy day or day off (a short walk or warming up and stretching)	Threshold (sustained effort for 20–25 minutes at 75–85% of HR$_{max}$)	Easy day or day off (a short walk or warming up and stretching)
LSD (20% of target mileage goal)	Easy day or day off (a short walk or warming up and stretching)	Threshold (5–6 intervals at 75–85% of HR$_{max}$)	Easy day or day off (a short walk or warming up and stretching)	Easy day or day off (a short walk or warming up and stretching)	Interval (3–4 intervals at 85–95% of HR$_{max}$)	Easy day or day off (a short walk or warming up and stretching)
LSD (20% of target mileage goal)	Easy day or day off (a short walk or warming up and stretching)	Interval (3–4 intervals at 85–95% of HR$_{max}$)	Threshold (sustained effort for 20–25 minutes at 75–85% of HR$_{max}$)	Easy day or day off (a short walk or warming up and stretching)	Easy day or day off (a short walk or warming up and stretching)	Threshold (5–6 intervals at 75–85% of HR$_{max}$)

Conclusion

For many people, simply walking a set route each and every day is completely satisfying. Doing so will bring about and maintain a certain level of fitness, and the consistency and dedication to that routine will provide many years of healthy living. However, for those who wish to push themselves to greater levels of performance, interval, threshold, and over-distance (LSD) training are the tools to make that increased performance a reality. While patience is most critical to training for performance, being committed to progressive overloading and creative workouts will return tremendous results.

In Practice

By now, you should have a good idea of where you want to take your fitness. In Chapter Six, you learned how strength training can help you improve your aerobic power and increase your stride length. In this chapter, you learned how you can use different types of aerobic training to improve those factors as well. Write down a short-term goal and then compose a four-week cardiovascular workout regimen to help you achieve that goal. Use the table provided to compose your workout.

Goal:

Sunday	Monday	Tuesday	Wednesday	Thursday	Friday	Saturday

WALKING FOR WEIGHT LOSS

Introduction

When it comes to performance or the pursuit of fitness goals, one of the most important contributing components is nutrition. Likewise, nutrition is often one of the most perplexing variables in a person's pursuit of health and fitness. It is important to understand that there are many different views on what is appropriate nutrition, and different people will have better success than others with specific diet plans. It is also important to note that calorie-restricting programs (often referred to as diets) work in the short term. However, the best way to lose and maintain weight and body fat is to follow a structured yet variable diet. The goals of this chapter are to deliver general nutrition knowledge, provide direction on how to generate a negative caloric balance, and discuss aspects of sports nutrition.

Nutrition Basics

Proper nutrition revolves around the balance of macronutrients and micronutrients. Macronutrients, also known as substrates, are those nutrients that can provide energy. The macronutrients are carbohydrate, fat, and protein, and each is made up of carbon, hydrogen, and oxygen. The micronutrients are commonly known as vitamins and minerals. Micronutrients are responsible for assisting in metabolism and cellular maintenance. A diet that is well balanced with appropriate macronutrients is sure to help meet an individual's micronutrient needs; therefore, this section will focus only on macronutrients.

Carbohydrates are the preferred energy source for the body. Carbohydrates are easily digested and stored as glycogen in the muscles and the liver. As well, a small percentage of the body's carbohydrate is contained in the blood as glucose. All told, an average male stores approximately 500 grams (2000 calories) of carbohydrate in his body, when fully loaded. At a moderately high intensity, those are enough calories to keep that man performing for approximately two hours. However, given that the man cannot eat a large meal within a few hours of his event (more about this later in the chapter), and given that some calories will be used up in the warm-up process, this man will not be at full capacity for carbohydrate stores. The second-most preferred source of energy is fat. Excepting those who have dangerously low body fat percentages, most people have enough fat stored in their bodies to endure very long exercise sessions. However, there is much more that goes into substrate utilization than appears in those very generalized statements.

One of the preferred measures of metabolic activity is the respiratory exchange ratio (RER or R). R is the ratio of the average of expired CO_2 to inspired O_2 or VCO_2/VO_2. The ratio ranges between 0.70 and 1.00, although ratios of slightly greater than 1.00 can be achieved during near exhaustive exercise, due to hyperventilation. Fats are burned through oxidation, which is also known as aerobic metabolism (burning calories with the use of oxygen), and pure oxidation of fats will result in an R of

0.70. The only time that is likely to happen, however, is when someone is in basal metabolism, which occurs when comatose or in deep sleep. In other words, if one is awake, the R will be greater than 0.70. Simply, that means that there is, almost always, a combination of fats and carbohydrate being burned.

More importantly, by monitoring different modes of exercise at various levels of intensity, we know that even low-intensity exercise will lead to an R close to 0.80. Therefore, we know that to burn fat, we also are burning carbohydrate, which means that the limited supply of carbohydrate will eventually run out. As we exercise at higher intensities, the R goes up, indicating a greater reliance on carbohydrate, leading to a quicker depletion of the substrate. Therefore, carbohydrate supplementation is essential to continued performance during exercise sessions that are expected to last 90 minutes or more, especially when intensities will generate heart rates of 80% of HR_{max} or higher.

Despite their important role in providing energy for activity, carbohydrates have been blacklisted in several nutrition circles, including in sports nutrition. Those blacklists have led to many calling for people to follow low-carbohydrate diets. Much of the push for low-carbohydrate diets comes as a result of the body's incredible ability to preserve itself. When carbohydrate stores get low, the body can produce carbohydrate through the process known as gluconeogenesis, which is the production of glucose from non-carbohydrate sources (fats, proteins, and other substances). It is during this time that proteins become an energy substrate, for during normal metabolic conditions, proteins are spared for use in their more important roles of building muscles, providing structural support in other tissues, as building blocks for enzymes and antibodies, and for storage. More importantly, the sugars made through gluconeogenesis cannot be metabolized by the brain and spinal cord, meaning that unless glucose is made available, the central nervous system function will decrease, leading to less muscle stimulus and decreased performance. You often see that when you see an ultra-endurance athlete hit "the wall" and stumble the remaining few hundred meters to the finish line.

The natural question arises as to why carbohydrates, having such importance and not being completely replaceable, have been so heavily discredited. Much of the problem started in the late 1980s into the 1990s, when Americans heavily emphasized fat-free diets. The popular mantra was to eat carbohydrate-based foods because there was very little fat in them, if at all. People began eating large portions of pasta and fat-free versions of traditionally "fatty" foods such as cheeses, yogurts, and candies. Eat all you want, some would say, as there was no, or almost no, fat in the foods.

Three very important failures occurred in that era, however. First, portion sizes were largely ignored. Because there was little fat in the foods, it was considered alright to eat as much as one wanted. While fat has more than twice as many calories per gram as carbohydrate, there are still calories in the latter. Eating more calories than you burn, regardless of whether they come from carbohydrate, fat, or protein, will result in the excess calories being stored as fat. Second, fats provide satiety in foods, and satiety means that a person's appetite is satisfied with less food. Additionally, being satiated means that the satisfaction remains longer. By taking away the fats, people were not becoming satisfied as quickly, meaning that they ate more, and they returned for more food more quickly as well. This lead to overconsumption and increased body fat stores. Finally, in an attempt to create low-fat foods with greater satiety and better taste, food manufacturers were loading the foods with sugars, making the foods very calorie dense and very high in simple sugars. As will be discussed in greater detail over the next few paragraphs, simple sugars break down very quickly, and they enter the bloodstream in concentrations much higher than can be handled through uptake into muscles and the liver, so the excess is stored as fat. In short, people overate carbohydrate, and they overate the wrong kinds of carbohydrate. The result was that they gained body fat.

Carbohydrates are in many of the foods we eat, but not all carbohydrates are created equally. For the most part, carbohydrates should be eaten relative to their position in the glycemic index (GI). The GI is a scale that rates carbohydrate based on the rapidity of digestion and absorption into the blood stream. The higher the GI rating is, the more rapid will be the absorption. When absorbed into the bloodstream too quickly, and in large quantities, the body cannot release insulin fast enough to shuttle the sugar from the blood into muscle. Instead, the sugars are converted to fat. The GI is based on glucose being rated the highest (100) on the scale, and foods with GI of 70 or more are often targeted as being foods to avoid (e.g. sodas, sports drinks, potatoes [sweet {albeit on the border of a moderate GI} and white], high-fructose corn syrup, white bread, bagels, and white rice [most types]). In contrast, foods with low GI (e.g. beans, most whole grains, fruits such as peaches and strawberries, and most nuts) are emphasized for healthier diets. Because of their GI rating, many beneficial foods, such as tomatoes, carrots, grapes, raisins, bananas, and sweet potatoes, are eliminated from diets.

Certainly, it is in one's best interests to limit high-glycemic foods. That is especially true for those that are in liquid form, as they need no mechanical digestion and can be absorbed into the bloodstream almost immediately, leading to excessive blood glucose concentrations and increased fat stores. As well, chronic consumption of high-GI foods stimulates regular, rapid increases in insulin, which can lead to insulin resistance and type 2 diabetes. Despite the drawbacks associated with high-GI foods, they do not have to be avoided completely.

In order to reap the benefits of higher GI foods, one simply needs to slow down their absorption. For example, sweet potatoes are terrific sources of fiber, Vitamins A and C, and calcium, but they have a GI of 70. Many will dress their sweet potatoes with butter and plenty of cinnamon sugar, which do little for altering the GI. When paired with dinner rolls, a protein, and soda, the dressed sweet potato will be absorbed rather quickly (as will the rolls and soda). However, an undressed sweet potato as a side to a main course of grilled fish on a bed of whole grain rice with mushrooms, and paired with lemon-infused water, makes for a meal that will be absorbed much more moderately. As well, that meal would provide a balance of carbohydrate, protein, and fat, in addition to fiber, calcium, iron, and all of the essential vitamins. A vegetarian could combine the sweet potato with tri-colored bell peppers and black beans, sautéed in balsamic vinegar, with a side of fresh pineapple, for a tasty, moderately low-GI dinner that would also pair well with a lemon-infused water. A good way to ensure that one is getting mostly good carbohydrate is to limit the intake of sugars to 30% of the total carbohydrate intake for the day.

Like carbohydrates, there are good and less good sources of fats, as well. Fats are classified as saturated and unsaturated, with the latter being further reduced to those that are mono- and poly-unsaturated. For a fat to be saturated, each of its carbons must be fully saturated with hydrogen

© Shutterstock/Marcos Mesa Sam Wordley

Figure 8.1 While carbohydrates are essential for proper fueling of the body, including the brain and muscles, limiting simple sugars, like in sodas, is critical for healthy body composition.

(hydrogen takes up all of the available valence electron spaces in the carbon, thereby linking the hydrogen to the carbon). Saturated fats are very stable; thus, they are solid at room temperatures. Mono- and poly-unsaturated fats are those that have one or more carbons that are uncovered by hydrogen, and they are liquid at room temperatures. Trans fats, also known as hydrogenated fats, are mono- or poly-unsaturated fats into which are forced additional hydrogen ions, thereby giving them the properties of saturated fats, but actually making them harder to break down and more dangerous to the cardiovascular system (e.g. margarine). A best practice is to limit trans fats as much as possible, but as a whole, trans fats and saturated fats should not exceed 30% of one's daily fat intake.

Protein needs, for most, are less complicated, as most meat eaters get plenty of protein in their diets. In fact, most Americans get sufficient protein if they are getting between 0.80 and 1.20 grams (g) of protein per kilogram (kg [pounds divided by 2.2]) of body weight. More athletically inclined persons will need to be at 1.20 to 1.98 g/kg, with most people who are walking for fitness being at the low end of that scale (1.20 to 1.30 g/kg). For example, a 130-pound female (130/2.2 = 59 kg) who walks about five miles per day will likely need 1.3 g/kg of protein for a total of 76.8 g of protein per day. One can get almost half of that protein from one four-ounce serving of grilled chicken (~36 g protein). For vegetarians, protein needs can be harder to satisfy, as non-animal sources of protein are incomplete. An incomplete protein is the one that does not contain all of the essential amino acids (those amino acids that cannot be made by the human body itself). Therefore, vegetarians must eat combinations of foods that contain the different essential amino acids (such as beans combined with rice) in order to get complete proteins.

While protein needs can be determined based on activity levels and body weight, it is important to meet the needs for all macronutrients. A number of diets exist, out there, that tell the reader that he or she needs to augment calories from one macronutrient while limiting the calories from another. However, most diets are not founded on good scientific research principles. Instead, many diets are based on theories that might work for limited groups of people for limited periods of time, but they frequently end in frustration for the dieter.

Following an eating plan such as Weight Watchers or Nutrisystem can be rewarding, as the former teaches portion control and caloric balance through a point system and the latter provides pre-determined meals that control portions and calories. The concern with Weight Watchers is the reality that the dieter makes the decisions as to how to use his or her points, so he or she can use those points for foods that are not overly nutritious rather than using them for healthier options. In the end, if the points are honored, the dieter will lose weight, but not in a long-lasting or beneficial manner. Likewise, a person needs to be dedicated to sticking to the restrictive portions of the Nutrisystem diet in order to lose weight, and that can be difficult for many.

There are several other diet plans that teach sensible eating habits. The South Beach Diet emphasizes lean, heart healthy proteins combined with lower glycemic carbohydrates that control blood sugar levels. My Plate emphasizes portion control and a diet balanced among fruits, vegetables, proteins, grains, and dairy. Because balance is of great importance, diets that deemphasize any macronutrient should be avoided.

Taking away from the last two paragraphs, it may be clear that the word diet is often misconstrued. When most hear the word diet, they think of caloric restriction with the intent of losing weight. However, in a more general, and accurate depiction, diet represents that which the person ingests, often regulated by thoughtfully planned meals. If one desires to lose fat weight, he or she needs to plan to ingest fewer calories than he or she expends. If one is looking to gain weight, he or she must take in more calories than he or she expends (combined with working out, if the desire is to gain muscle weight). In the end, there is no magic diet that will get one where he or she desires to be. Instead, the emphasis should be on taking in a balanced diet that limits simple sugars and saturated fats.

Figure 8.2 The South Beach Diet balances lean proteins, mainly fish, with colorful vegetables and low- to moderate-GI carbohydrates.

Figure 8.3 My Plate has made balanced nutrition easier to determine and less intimidating.

The 60–20–20 Diet Recommendation

While there are many diet plans out there for a person to follow, the best ratio of macronutrients is 60% carbohydrate, 20% fat, and 20% protein. This ratio is well supported by exercise physiology and the study of macronutrient metabolism. Additionally, as was presented in this chapter, sugars should account for no more than 30% of the carbohydrate allotment, and saturated and trans fats should account for no more than 30% of the fat allotment. Let's take Jill, a recreational walker, who weighs 130 pounds and walks seven days a week at a moderate pace for one hour. Jill needs 2,080 calories per day (see Figure 8.2) in order to maintain her body weight. Therefore, Jill should be getting 1,248 calories (312 grams) from carbohydrate, but no more than 374 (93.5 grams) of those calories should come from simple sugars. Jill should also consume approximately 416 calories (46 grams) from fat of which no more than 125 calories (13.8 grams) should be saturated or trans fats. That leaves Jill with another 416 calories (104 grams) from protein.

We know from earlier in this chapter that Jill's protein needs can be calculated more precisely. She is active, but she is also female, meaning that she is not likely to be highly muscular. We also know that her activity is primarily in the form of recreational walking, which is not a high-intensity exercise. Therefore, Jill probably needs the upper end of the protein requirements for an average person, which is also the lower end of the protein requirements for an athlete, 1.2 grams of protein per kilogram of body weight. Jill's weight in kilograms is 59.09 kg, so her more precise protein requirements are 1.2 g × 59.09 kg, meaning Jill really only needs 71 grams (284 calories) of protein, 33 grams fewer than calculated by the 60–20–20 ratio. That would leave Jill with 132 calories that she can use elsewhere. If Jill wants to lose a little fat, she could not ingest those calories (see *Caloric Balance* below), and she would lose a pound of fat in approximately 26.5 days. If Jill wants to maintain her 130 pounds, her best move would be to add those 132 calories to her fat allotment, allowing her another 14.5 grams of fat in her diet (she'll need it for her long walks).

In the end, Jill would either end up on a 60–26–14 ratio or a 64–21–15 ratio, if she were to maintain the 2080 calories or lose the 132 calories, respectively. Both ratios are perfectly acceptable, leaving Jill with the freedom of choice.

Figure 8.4 Water is essential for proper digestion, organ function, temperature regulation, and more. Adults should consume from 64 to 96 ounces of water per day.

In addition to needing sufficient macronutrients and micronutrients, humans must meet one other essential nutrition need, fluid balance. When we sweat, we lose fluid. When we breath, we lose water. Therefore, regular rehydration is essential to maintaining fluid balance. Without proper fluid balances in our bodies, our metabolism, thermoregulation, circulation, musculoskeletal function, waste removal, and cellular integrity are all compromised. For most, consuming 64 ounces of water per day is adequate, and the emphasis should be on water, trying to limit the consumption of sodas (regular and diet), highly caffeinated drinks, and alcohol. As well, grossly hyper-hydrating, as is commonly seen in those who drink a gallon (128 ounces) of water or more per day, is not advised. Doing so can lead to a state of hyponatremia, in which critical, water-soluble vitamins (the B vitamins and vitamin C) and minerals can be flushed from the body. Hyponatremia can lead to compromised immunity, muscular contractility issues (including the heart), and decreased metabolism.

Caloric Balance

There is considerably more to good nutrition than eating a balance of macronutrients and maintaining proper hydration. Many turn to nutrition for satisfying weight and body fat goals, and nutrition practices are critically important to gaining, losing, or maintaining weight and body fat. If one is providing his or her body with a balance of carbohydrate, fat, and protein, the methods for achieving weight and body fat goals are relatively simple. If one wants to lose weight, he or she needs to burn more calories than he or she takes in. If one wants to maintain weight, he or she needs to take in calories equal in number to those expended. If one wants to gain weight, he or she needs to make a decision of whether that weight will be in the form of fat or muscle. For the former, the simple answer is to ingest more calories than are expended each day. For the latter, more calories will need to be consumed, but they need to be measured, and there must be a conscientious effort to increase exercise by way of the FIT-M principle. In other words, to gain muscle, one must increase exercise frequency, intensity, and time, or a combination of any of those, while providing the calories needed to refuel and rebuild the muscles.

On paper, losing fat is relatively easy. In order to lose a pound of fat, one must consume 3,500 fewer calories than he or she expends. The safe recommendation is to lose no more than two pounds per week, with the more conservative approach being no more than one pound per week. For the latter, the daily caloric deficit needs to be 500 calories lost per day. More aggressively, losing two pounds per week would require a net loss of 1,000 calories per day. In the end, it does not matter where the short-coming comes. If one needs 2,000 calories per day to maintain his or she weight, he or she could simply shave off 500 calories and drop his or her daily allotment to 1,500. This would require adjusting the macronutrient balance accordingly, as well (it is highly recommended that no one ever goes below 1,500 calories per day). If one needs 2,000 calories per day and does not want to give up carbohydrates, he or she could drop 500 calories (99 grams) of fat from his or her diet, or drop 500 calories between fat and protein. Another option would be to not change caloric intake at all, and achieve the net loss of calories by way of increasing caloric expenditure by 500 calories (approximately an extra 30 minutes of exercise per day). Finally, the net loss could come from a combination of increased exercise and caloric restriction, which is definitely the proper course of action if trying to lose more than one pound of fat per week.

A sure fire way to help one's body lose fat weight is to take advantage of its thermogenic principles. Think of the body as a wood-burning fireplace. When the fire first gets going, it burns rapidly and hot. However, as the wood turns to coals and ash, the fire dies down, as does the heat. Knowing this, it's instinctive to throw another log or two on the fire, prior to it turning to coals, and the rapid, hot flames strike back up. As long as the desire is for the flames to burn hot, one needs to feed the fire.

The human body operates in the same fashion. Everyone has heard the notion that breakfast is the most important meal of the day, and it is. If one eats his or her last meal at 8:00 PM, goes to bed at 11:00 PM, and sleeps until 6:00 AM, it is likely to be close to 12 hours, or half a day, since his or her last meal. With that length of time, sugar stores are lessened considerably, and the body is in a state of resting metabolism. Providing the body with new energy is like starting the fire all over again, and one is ready for the day. The big mistake comes when the next meal comes five or six hours later, at lunch, and then another five or six hours later at dinner. The flames will die down, and the metabolic fire will quell. However, with breakfast at 7:00 AM, a snack at 10:00 AM, lunch at 1:00 PM, a snack at 3:00 PM, dinner at 6:00 PM, and another snack at 8:00 PM, the flames never completely die out, and the metabolic furnace burns hot all day. When that happens, the body naturally burns more calories. Take note that while one is eating often, he or she will also feel hungry more often, as the body will be looking for more calories to maintain the increased metabolism.

By eating meals and snacks throughout the day, a second important physiological event occurs. For a person who needs 2,000 calories a day, a typical three-meal caloric breakdown might be 800 calories for breakfast and 600 calories each for lunch and dinner. In the United States, that is often more like 400 calories for breakfast, 600 for lunch, and 1,000 for dinner, which is even worse. Physiologically, it is fairly well known that meals nearing 1,000 calories are more difficult for the body to digest, and less efficient digestion can lead to increased body fat. Meals of approximately 500 calories, however, are efficiently digested, regardless of age or sex. That same 2,000 calories split over three meals and three snacks will promote efficient digestion along with the higher metabolic rate. Those 2,000 calories broken down might look like 500–600 calories for breakfast, 200 calories for snack one, 500 calories for lunch, 200 calories for snack two, 400–500 calories for dinner, and 100 calories for snack three.

In trying to strike a caloric balance, it is important to accurately determine one's caloric needs. There are multiple ways in which to do this. First, assuming that his or her weight does not change, a person can log all calories ingested for a week and average those calories for a daily need. That method requires meticulous notetaking and accurate measurement of the foods taken in. The second method is to estimate caloric needs based on a formula that considers weight, sex, physical activity, and diet. The formula and an example of how to apply the formula is presented in *The Metabolic Equation*.

The Metabolic Equation

Determining caloric needs can be as easy as a simple math equation and a little logic. The equation requires the input of weight and consideration of physical activity levels and caloric balance of one's diet.

Total Caloric Need = Basal Metabolic Rate (BMR) + Physical Activity (PA) + Thermal Effect of Food (TEF)

BMR = Body weight in pounds × 10 (for women) or × 11 (for men)

PA = BMR × 0.25 (low physical activity levels [<60 minutes of moderate physical activity per day]), × 0.50 (moderate activity levels [60–120 minutes of physical activity per day]), or × .75 (high-activity levels [>2 hours of moderately high physical activity per day])

TEF = BMR × 0.10 (for a diet rich in carbohydrates) or × 0.05 (for a diet rich in fats)

Using this formula, let's calculate the caloric needs of Jill, a 130-pound woman who walks 60 minutes per day, seven days per week, and eats a high-carbohydrate diet.

BMR = Body weight in lbs. × 10 = 130 lbs. × 10 calories/lb. = 1300 calories

PA = BMR × 0.50 (for moderate activity of 60–120 minutes) = 1300 × 0.50 = 650 calories

TEF = BMR × 0.10 (for a carbohydrate-rich diet) = 1300 × 0.10 = 130 calories

Jill's total caloric need = 1300 + 650 + 130 = 2080 total calories

Eating for Performance and Recovery

Pre- and post-workout nutrition is an important consideration. While an exercise routine of walking 30–60 minutes per day does not require any special pre- or post-workout nutrition planning, some principles of sports nutrition may still be of value. More importantly, for those who might seek to engage in walking activities that are of higher intensity or longer duration, proper sports nutrition is critical to the optimal completion of the activities.

A pre-workout meal is critical to maximizing performance, especially in endurance events or those of high intensity. Therefore, who are considering walking in a competitive event, from a 5K to a marathon, need to consider what they eat both before and after the competition. Likewise, pre-workout nutrition must be considered prior to performing any of the workouts listed in Chapter Seven.

Pre-competition nutrition is relative to the length of the competition. A person who intends to walk a marathon will need to ensure that his or her muscle and liver glycogen stores are fully loaded. Thus, the practice of carbohydrate loading (carbo-loading) is essential. Carbo-loading can be achieved through any one of the following three methods. Traditional loading requires that the person perform a glycogen-depleting workout seven days prior to the goal competition. Over the next seven days, the person eats a carbohydrate-rich diet (carbohydrate percentages of 60% or more in the diet). Concurrently, the person must lessen his or her exercise to decrease caloric expenditure. A second method of carbo-loading is to follow the same guidelines as traditional loading, only performing them over a four-day period, rather than seven days. Finally, a third method is to simply decrease exercise over a seven-day period while eating a high-carbohydrate diet.

Shorter events do not require carbo-loading, but a pre-competition or pre-workout (pre-event) meal is still essential for maximum performance. Likewise, pre-competition meals are critical to the success of longer distance events, as well. Timing of these meals is critical. Pre-event meals should be consumed two to three hours prior to the event. The given time length allows the meal to be digested and absorbed into bloodstream where the glycogen can be stored in both the muscles and liver.

There are two additional reasons that the timing of pre-event meals is essential. First, once a person begins exercising, blood is shunted from the splanchnic region (abdominal/digestive area) in order to provide greater blood flow to the working muscles. The decreased blood flow leads to a substantial decrease in function, thereby making digestion a very low priority. Therefore, during exercise, it is best to limit dietary intake to liquids that can be easily absorbed from the digestive tract. Second, during bouts of exercise, the body uses a more direct method of shuttling glucose into muscle tissue, the Glut-4 receptor protein. The encoded Glut-4 proteins provide a channel by which glucose moves into the muscle cell. As an important regulatory event, the activation of the Glut-4 receptors provides negative feedback to the pancreas to quell the release of insulin. However, because of the slow nature of insulin secretion, if a substance is ingested within 30–45 minutes of exercise, there will likely be an overlap of Glut-4 and insulin actions. With both insulin and Glut-4 receptors shuttling glucose into the muscle, blood sugar levels will drop below normal levels (hypoglycemia), causing a lack of sugar to be available for the brain. The lack of sugar to the brain will decrease brain function, leading to decreased muscular function, cognition, and physical performance.

The two important physiological conditions related to glucose digestion and uptake not only demonstrate the need for appropriate pre-event eating but also provide the rationale for maintaining blood glucose and muscle glycogen levels during exercise. As stated in the previous paragraph, liquid-type "foods" (liquids and gels) should be ingested during exercise. The ability of the body to digest the liquids makes the substrates in them more readily absorbable and the probability of stomach discomfort is lessened. As well, because blood sugar levels must be maintained, energy supplementation should be done in small amounts, frequently throughout the exercise.

Post-exercise or recovery nutrition is every bit as important as pre-event nutrition. After exercise, the body seeks to restock the muscles with glycogen and protein. Glycogen replacement allows the muscles to continue to remain metabolic after the exercise session is completed (depending on intensity, post-exercise metabolism can remain elevated for upward of six hours), while also allowing the muscles to be fueled up for their next use. Protein, in the form of amino acids, is used to start healing micro-tears that occur when muscles are overloaded. Repair of the micro-tears brings about muscular hypertrophy and increased performance.

It is important to take advantage of timing in recovery nutrition as well. Within the first 15 minutes of recovery, a liquid recovery drink should be consumed. The liquid nature allows the substrates to be rapidly absorbed, and the proximity to exercise allows the body to take advantage of the still active Glut-4 receptors. Unlike the carbohydrate-rich solutions one should drink during exercise, the recovery drink should be a combination of carbohydrate and protein, with calorie concentrations being about 5/8 carbohydrate and 3/8 protein. The recovery drink should be fairly low in calories, with approximately 120–150 calories being sufficient. Within two hours after the exercise session has ended, a carbohydrate-rich meal should be eaten. That meal should be roughly 400–500 calories, allowing for further refueling of the muscles and liver.

Conclusion

Nutrition is a very complex science. However, one's personal nutrition can be largely controlled by maintaining an appropriate balance among carbohydrate, fat, and protein, and by eating the recommended amount of calories for one's body size and physical activity levels. Additionally, when seeking peak performance in competitions or workouts, pre- and post-event meals can provide the energy for that workout and those to follow.

As a final consideration, maintaining good nutrition habits requires monitoring, review, and revision. There are many nutrition-tracking applications for computers and smart phones, and several of those allow the user to scan the food's barcode for immediate uploading of all pertinent information. Food databases provide macronutrient and micronutrient information on most common foods. Maintaining a food-tracking journal is the best way to ensure that one is eating the appropriate percentages of macronutrients as well as staying on target for meeting caloric needs. While time consuming, food logs make personal nutrition much easier to master.

In Practice

It's important to have an understanding of your caloric needs and intakes. Generally speaking, a review of nutrition intakes and outputs should happen over several days. For this exercise, however, you will review one day of your normal nutrition. First, use the metabolic equation provided in this chapter to determine your caloric needs. Second, eating as you would normally eat, log the total calories and macronutrients you consume in an entire day, breaking your evaluation down meal-by-meal. Report your findings here.

$$BMR = \underset{\text{weight in pounds}}{\underline{\hspace{2cm}}} \times \underset{\text{coefficient}}{\underline{\hspace{1.5cm}}} = \underset{\text{total calories}}{\underline{\hspace{1.5cm}}}$$

$$PA = \underset{\text{BMR}}{\underline{\hspace{2cm}}} \times \underset{\text{coefficient}}{\underline{\hspace{1.5cm}}} = \underset{\text{total calories}}{\underline{\hspace{1.5cm}}}$$

$$TEF = \underset{\text{BMR}}{\underline{\hspace{2cm}}} \times \underset{\text{coefficient}}{\underline{\hspace{1.5cm}}} = \underset{\text{total calories}}{\underline{\hspace{1.5cm}}}$$

$$\text{Total Caloric Need} = \underset{\text{BMR}}{\underline{\hspace{1cm}}} + \underset{\text{PA}}{\underline{\hspace{1.5cm}}} + \underset{\text{TEF}}{\underline{\hspace{1cm}}} = \underset{\text{total calories}}{\underline{\hspace{1.5cm}}}$$

Meal	Fat Calories	Carbohydrate Calories	Protein Calories	Total Calories
Breakfast				
Time:				
Lunch				
Time:				
Dinner				
Time:				
Snack 1				
Time:				
Snack 2				
Time:				
Snack 3				
Time				
Daily Total				

Your analysis:_____
_____
_____
_____
_____

THE WALKING LIFESTYLE

Introduction

It takes a substantial commitment to walk on a regular basis, especially when other aspects of life can get in the way. There is no denying the importance and significance of that dedication, and those who walk regularly should take pride in their accomplishments. However, as the previous eight chapters have demonstrated, while getting in a regular walk is important, there is considerably more to the fitness walking lifestyle than walking.

The fitness walking lifestyle requires a balance of training, proper nutrition, flexibility training, and evaluation of one's fitness. To take on such a lifestyle is a responsibility that takes some time to get used to. It also takes considerable planning as well as the support of others.

In order to maintain a healthy lifestyle, no matter what is at the center of it, one needs to have a high degree of self-efficacy. Self-efficacy, a concept penned by Stanford University's Dr. Albert Bandura, is one's confidence in his or her ability to bring about a behavior and maintain it. In order to develop self-efficacy, a person needs to be educated, well trained, goal oriented, and composed.

© Shutterstock/Photobank Gallery

Figure 9.1 A group might be able to take an individual to heights he might not believe he can achieve on his own.

As well, the more successes a person has, the more confidence he or she will gain. Self-efficacy also relies on self-reliance and a high degree of intrinsic motivation, qualities not everyone possesses.

When a high degree of self-efficacy is not present in an individual, he or she can fall back on another concept, group, or collective efficacy. Collective efficacy is a group's assurance that, as a whole, it can maintain a behavior. The beauty of collective efficacy is that individuals of different backgrounds will contribute different strengths to the group, and those combined strengths will provide the group with the tools necessary to maintain the desired behaviors. In that way, there is less reliance on self, and belonging to the group provides high levels of extrinsic motivation.

Regardless of the type of efficacy, two common factors must be acknowledged. Those are setting goals and maintaining motivation. This chapter focuses on the methods of manipulating those two factors in ways that facilitate a permanent, healthy lifestyle.

Goal Setting

The best way to achieve an end is to have an appropriate means to that end. In other words, there needs to be a clear path that leads one from the starting point to the final destination. For example, when writing an essay, it's always recommended that one starts with an outline, which then guides the creative writing process. A better example would be the construction of a house. Considerable time is spent in grading the land and laying the foundation, followed by the external walls, then the roof, the internal walls, and so on. Each progressive step gets the builder closer to completion of the house, until it is finally completed. If the builder had skipped a step, the house might have looked complete, but it would likely have collapsed before it could be sold to a prospective owner.

Like the house in the analogy, a lifestyle that is built on a proper foundation and follows an appropriate plan can last indefinitely. In contrast, a lifestyle that follows no specific direction will often falter, and its full potential left unrealized. Lifestyle changes must happen in well-defined steps, each one is more progressive than the one before.

Goal setting is a process that is often taken lightly. For example, the most popular day for setting goals is New Year's Day, when millions will make ill-fated resolutions. Unfortunately, for many people, those resolutions are approached without the proper foundation being laid, and most of them are broken before the New Year is two weeks old. Often, it is not that the resolution was not important to the person, nor is it that the resolution was unattainable. Instead, the resolutions are stated in very grand terms (e.g. I'm going to lose 50 pounds this year) or the person making the resolution lacks the resources to make the resolution a reality (e.g. a single parent who targets earning a college a degree only to realize that she has no one to care for her kids while she's in class).

When it comes to fitness walking, many walkers establish goals of losing weight, while others want to increase cardiovascular health. However, both of those goals, and many others like them, take a long time to realize. While long-term goals help to establish an ultimate destination for one's fitness endeavors, short-term goals provide the intermediate benchmarks that allow a person to check progress and evaluate the steps being taken to reach the long-term goal. If a short-term goal is not met in the desired timeframe, or if it is exceeded, the exerciser will be able to adjust accordingly.

Like the linear periodization model, discussed in Chapter Six, goal setting should get an exerciser from a baseline measure to the anticipated outcome in a structured and logical pattern of progression. Unlike linear periodization, goals rarely express an anticipated decrease in performance. However, if progress is checked frequently, the exerciser can reestablish his or her short-term goals in order to establish a detour that will get him or her back on track toward the long-term goal.

As was previously suggested, long-term goals must be realistic and appropriate for the desired change. Short-term goals must also be realistic and appropriate; only the short-term goals do not necessarily reflect the desired change. Instead, short-term goals should reflect components of the change. Regardless of their being long- or short-term goals, all goal setting should follow these guidelines:

Figure 9.2 To effectively satisfy a long-term goal, short-term goals must be progressive yet attainable.

- Goals need to be precise (be as specific as possible in terms of how, where, and when).
- Goals must be attainable (e.g. it is very realistic to lose a pound per week, but it is unrealistic and dangerous to assume that weight loss of much more than one pound per week is appropriate).
- Goals must be measureable (relating back to the first bullet, each goal should be quantifiable [measurable with numbers] or quantitatively measured [subjective evaluation]).
- Goals must be written down. There is something about putting things in writing to help hold oneself accountable.
- Goals should be posted conspicuously (or communicated to someone else). While some goals may not be the type of material that one would want others to know, goals that can be posted where others can see them can lead to conversations that reinforce the behavior.

Effective goal setting requires an in-depth understanding of the factors that impact the long-term goal(s) in question. To that end, research is fundamental to developing appropriate long- and short-term goals. With respect to walking, one should seek to understand how the body adapts to walking (as discussed in the earlier chapters of this book). One might research what resources are available, such as existing walking clubs, discovering safe walking routes, and finding stores that provide equipment, foods, and clothing to support the lifestyle.

Tip 9.1

So often, individuals will begin following a walking regimen in order to lose weight. However, frustration often sets in, as the weight does not immediately start dropping, and it can often increase with each day a pound is not lost. It takes time to lose body fat, and acute exercise can often lead to temporary water retention as well as a gain in muscle size (hypertrophy), both of which increase body weight. The best advice one can heed when starting a workout regimen is to weigh on the first day of the program and then not step foot on the scale again for months. Instead, pay attention to variables that are more indicative of change. Are your clothes fitting more loosely? Do you feel more energized? Are you getting better sleep at night?

Appropriate goals provide feedback and motivation that are important to self-efficacy. As such, a strong set of short- and long-term goals may be all that a highly intrinsically motivated person may need to be successful in maintaining a fitness walking lifestyle. However, most are not intrinsically motivated to that degree, and they may need a considerable amount of help to remain motivated to achieve such a lifestyle.

Staying Motivated

It is very difficult to maintain a health-and-wellness-based lifestyle. Social media, television, peer pressure, work and family obligations, and an environment stressing convenience (fast food drive-thru restaurants, highly processed foods, video games, kiosk-generated movie rentals, etc.) are substantial influences pulling us away from healthy lifestyles. An "us against the world battle" to maintain a healthy lifestyle is not a fair fight; there are far too many variables in play. The good news is that we are not in these battles alone, not if we don't want to be.

Collective efficacy provides that a group of like-minded individuals can often achieve more than a single person. While self-efficacy expects that an individual will gain the skills necessary to successfully maintain a behavior, collective efficacy provides that experts in one area lead the group at certain points, while others with different skill sets might take the lead at other times. Further, when one member of the group is lacking resiliency, others can provide the necessary support to keep him or her moving toward his or her goal.

Perhaps the most important aspect of collective efficacy is the ability of the group to hold each and every group member accountable. When considering self-efficacy, the individual is held accountable by no one other than himself or herself. When experiencing a challenging day, the individual can rationalize taking a day off, as he or she only has to convince himself or herself that such action is in line with his or her stated goals. Should the same scenario play out again the next day, it will be even easier for the individual to justify not following the workout schedule yet again.

When left to reach fitness goals by himself or herself, a person is accountable to no one but himself or herself. Thus, it's easy to procrastinate without any consequences. However, incorporating even a second person into the equation increases the accountability tremendously. Generally speaking, a

Figure 9.3 One of the best examples of collective efficacy is the wolf pack. Acting as one unit with a common goal, there is almost nothing more formidable than a pack of wolves.

<table>
<tr><td>

━━━━ Tip 9.2 ━━━━

If looking for a personal trainer, do your homework! Look for a personal trainer with a degree in exercise science who is certified by a credible organization. ACE provides a basic certification, while organizations such as NSCA, ACSM, and NASM set the standard for more elite certifications. Don't be afraid to ask a trainer the hard questions, such as the system used for record keeping, philosophy, and to provide a list of references.

</td></tr>
</table>

person feels compelled to not let down another person, and that compulsion is a powerful tool in maintaining efficacy. For example, on a cold and blustery morning, a person who normally rolls out of bed at 6:00 AM to walk five miles might decide to put the walk off until after work, or not walk at all. However, if that same person is scheduled to meet a friend at the local park, neither individual will want to let the other down, and they are both likely to keep their appointments with the other.

More than just accountability, a workout partner provides motivation. Daily workouts often become so routine that they can lead to boredom, and boredom is one of the leading causes of life-style disengagement. A workout partner, who is complimentary to one's own style and personality, can provide a dynamic that prevents a workout from being boring or routine. Further, a workout partner should provide valuable feedback regarding exercise technique, a spotter for difficult or technically challenging exercises, and a confidant with whom one can discuss any concerns that life brings to the table. Finally, if amenable, a workout partner can be a source of competition that should bring out the best effort in each of you.

For those who prefer to remain singularly focused but need a higher level of accountability than themselves, a personal trainer is a terrific option. It can be quite costly to work with a personal trainer, and the fees charged by trainers will vary by each trainer's experience, education, credentials, and fitness facilities with whom the trainers are aligned. However, a once-a-week session with a trainer is a terrific way to keep oneself motivated and in check when it comes to established goals. Even a session per month can provide feedback that will help determine progress. In addition to the feedback and instruction received from a trainer, if one commits to paying for workout sessions, he or she is more likely to invest the time and energy to live a lifestyle that will support those workout sessions.

Yet another great source of motivation is to be part of a team. Certainly, not everyone can be part of a competitive team, and most who are reading this book are not seeking to join a race walking team. However, teams combine all of the features above in one nice neat package. First, the coach provides accountability as well as constructive feedback that should improve technique and fitness level. Second, the teammates will provide kinship that features a more symbiotic sense of accountability. Finally, with all of the different personalities that come together to form a single group, being part of a team is usually not boring.

In this case, a walking club can be a terrific substitute for a team. Walking clubs are fairly popular and prominent in most areas. However, if there is not a walking club in the area, it is an easy and relatively inexpensive to get one started. In order to be well informed of the clubs available, be sure to check out local sporting goods stores, malls (mall walker clubs are popular), and recreation departments.

Whether one decides to emphasize collective or self-efficacy in his or her lifestyle efforts, the important takeaway is to maintain a high degree of motivation. For some people, motivation will come in the form of the satisfaction that results from achieving milestones. For others, motivation might come from the change in appearance that will come from a fitness walking-based lifestyle. Others may need more tangible forms of motivation. Small rewards often provide the motivation required by those who are more extrinsically motivated. Examples of appropriate rewards include vacations (save long vacations for reaching a long-term goal), a pair of jeans that run a size smaller, a new exercise outfit or pair of shoes, or a night on the town. Tangible rewards are often the most effective form of reward, so it is not inappropriate to reward oneself with an item of value.

Conclusion

Living a lifestyle based on health and fitness takes considerable dedication. It is imperative to set realistic goals and to keep those goals progressing so as to provide continuous motivation to improve. However, motivation may also come from aligning oneself with others who share similar expectations. Monetary-based rewards are also useful tools to remain motivated. Perhaps it will take a combination of tools to motivate many who read this book.

Without well-conceived goals and holding oneself accountable for reaching them, a lifestyle steeped in health and wellness is truly not possible. Even if that lifestyle is not the goal, regular bouts of fitness walking will provide a higher quality of life, improved body composition, and a more viable cardiovascular system.

© Shutterstock/wavebreakmedia

Figure 9.4 Although they can be priced out of some peoples' budgets, personal trainers should be highly proficient at holding an individual accountable. If a trainer is not an option, pairing up with a training partner can be equally effective.

In Practice

After reading this book, you can see that there are many variables that factor into improving fitness walking performance and developing a lifestyle dedicated to improved health and fitness. Think of how far you have come over the course of this class, and think about where you would like to be six months from now. To that end, write one long-term fitness walking-related goal that you would like to achieve at the end of six months. As well, provide at least two short-term goals that you expect to achieve to help you progress to that six-month goal.

In addition to your goals, provide at least two ways in which you expect to remain motivated over the next six months.

In stating both your goals and your motivations, be sure that your expectations are realistic and attainable. Make an additional copy of your goals and post them where you will be able to refer to them regularly, helping you remain focused.